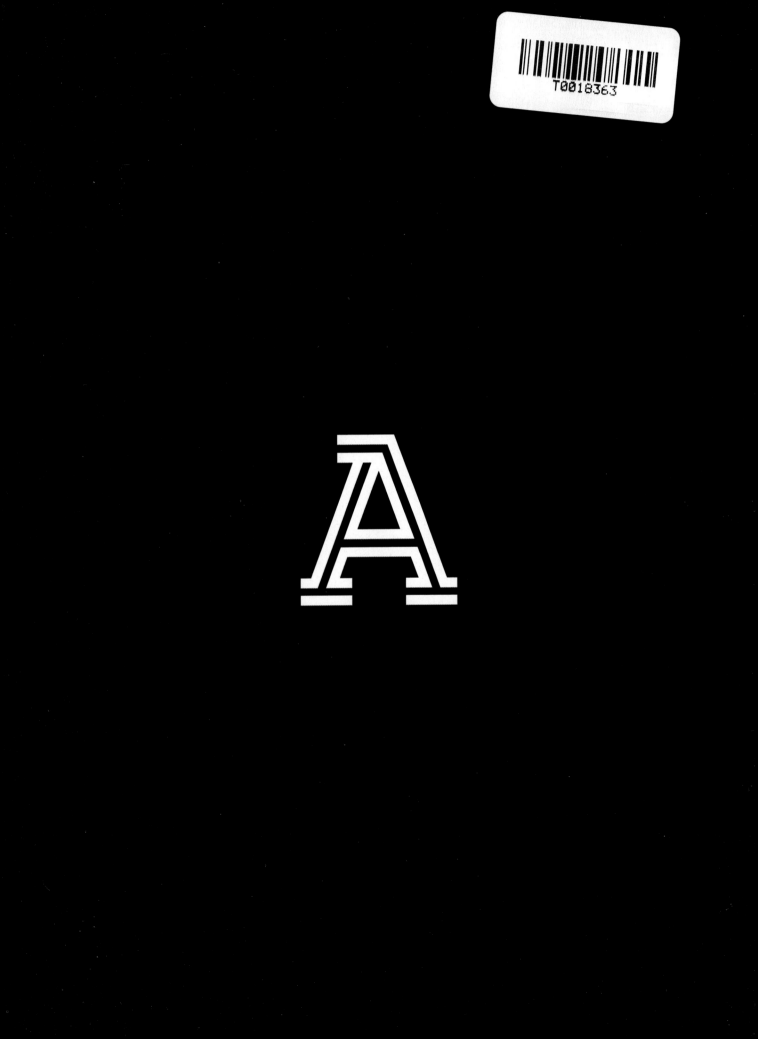

Contents

Introduction

By Sam Amick

It all started with Steph. The six NBA Finals appearances in eight years for this Golden State Warriors era that no one saw coming. The fourth championship, which they won on June 16, 2022, when his play in Game 6 was so sublime that he demanded another ring be put on his finger midway through the third quarter. The elation and affection that were there for all to see as the Warriors hoisted the trophy on the TD Garden floor and partied until the Boston sunrise neared.

Long before Wardell Stephen Curry II would inspire one of the most unique dynasties in league history, with his audacious shooting and selfless style setting the tone for the joyous journey that was to come alongside Klay Thompson, Draymond Green and all the rest, he was the wispy kid from Davidson who spent his early years at the next level living an underdog existence. His welcome-to-the-NBA moment came in 2009, when his backcourt mate, Monta Ellis, announced to reporters on media day that it would be impossible for them to play alongside one another and win.

"Just can't," Ellis famously said.

Curry was once benched for a journeyman named Acie Law — at the end of the veteran's underwhelming career, no less. He suffered through years of ankle injuries that made him wonder if he'd ever be able to truly shine in the pros. Forget about greatness. The notion of him being a productive, full-time starter was once in serious question.

And by the time the job against the Celtics was complete, with Curry winning his first Finals MVP in unanimous form after averaging 31.2 points, six rebounds, five assists and two steals, there was something poetic about the fact that his latest crown came in the same sort of against-all-odds fashion as his storied career began.

"Steph ultimately is why this run has happened," Warriors coach Steve Kerr said after Curry had 34 points, seven rebounds, seven assists and two steals in the Warriors' 103-90 win in the closeout game. "I'm happy for everybody, but I'm thrilled for Steph. To me this is his crowning achievement in what's already been an incredible career."

Make no mistake, this season was a far cry from the Kevin Durant years, when the Warriors entered every season as the heavy favorites. Though Golden State won two more games than the Celtics during the regular season, the Warriors lost 16 of 28 games in a brutal stretch run that was marred by injuries to Curry and Green after a sizzling 41-13 start.

Were they "Gold Blooded," as the team motto would later claim, or fool's gold? It looked like the latter by the time mid-February rolled around.

Thompson's early-January return from a two-year absence was the stuff of Hollywood scripts, as he'd battled back from the ACL tear he suffered in the 2019 finals and the Achilles tendon tear he endured a year later. But it also came with complications, and it was quickly apparent that the "Splash Brothers" storyline of old had been forever changed.

Not only did Thompson need time to find his sea legs again, but the Warriors had pivotal new players to take into consideration. Andrew Wiggins, the No. 1 pick who came their way in the D'Angelo Russell trade with Minnesota in February 2020, had blossomed on both ends under Warriors coach Steve Kerr and his staff. Jordan Poole, the high-scoring guard who was taken 28th out of Michigan in 2019, was quickly becoming a key piece of Golden State's new core. As all these roles and responsibilities changed, with the new players integrating with the old, questions about how this iteration of the Warriors would function emerged. A title run seemed wholly unlikely.

The Celtics, who started the season 23-24 only to boast the league's best record after Jan. 23 (28-7), enjoyed the inverse experience. And by the time the postseason arrived, when Boston boasted not only a No. 1-ranked defense, but also a core that had been to the conference finals in four of the past six seasons, the Celtics looked worthy of title-front-runner status.

Even with Curry playing well from the start of these finals, the Celtics still looked fully capable of finishing this job after their 116-100 win in Game 3 that gave them a 2-1 series lead. Like the Warriors, these Celtics were a defensive-minded, mostly homegrown group that was built to contend for the long haul. First-year coach Ime Udoka even spoke with reverence about everything the Warriors had been able to accomplish, while making it clear his team wanted nothing more than to replicate it.

"Six out of eight years (in the finals) for them is impressive, especially with some of the injuries they've been through," Udoka said before Game 3. "They've stayed consistent. It's a model for what we want to do here and build and grow into."

But Curry had other plans.

His Game 4 masterpiece — 43 points, 10 rebounds, seven 3-pointers — was arguably his finest moment on a finals stage. Curry howled at the raging Celtics fans early on, then kept his hot streak going until the very end.

The Warriors returned to their "Strength in Numbers" roots in Game 5, when Curry shot 7-of-22 overall and went 0-for-9 from 3-point range. Wiggins, Thompson, Gary Payton II, Poole — they all supplemented Curry's lack of scoring in the 104-94 Warriors win.

"I don't think I've ever been happier after a 0-for-whatever type of night," Curry said, "just knowing the context of the game, the other ways you tried to impact the game and the fact that, you know, you had four guys step up in meaningful ways. ... Yeah, there's a fire burning, and I want to make shots, but the rest of it is about how we win the game, and we did that."

Three days later, when the Warriors were back in front of that brutal Celtics crowd that resumed the "F*** Draymond" chants in the first quarter, Curry finished his best finals yet in emphatic form. With 6:15 left in the third quarter, he buried a 29-footer from the "NBA Finals" logo over Robert Williams and Marcus Smart to put the Warriors up 22, then pointed to his ring finger while staring into the stunned crowd.

The Celtics, who cut the lead to 10 entering the fourth quarter, weren't done just yet. But Curry, who had 13 of his 34 points in the fourth and gave his patented "night-night" gesture after his seventh and final 3 with 3:17 left, ended them for good from there.

It all ended with Steph, too.

As the final seconds ticked away, the 34-year-old was awash with emotion. With his hands on his head, he fell to the parquet floor and cried. Curry and the Warriors had done it — again.

"It was definitely overwhelming," Curry said. "It was surreal because you know how much you went through to get back to this stage, and nobody (understands), unless you've been on that floor, you just grind day-in and day-out.

"It all paid off. Didn't know how it was going to happen. Didn't know what the environment was going to be like. You imagine what the emotions are going to be like, but it hits different ....I just wanted to take in the moment because it was that special." ▬▬

A Matter of Intensity

Warriors Settle In for Physical Series Against Celtics

By Tim Kawakami

JUNE 6, 2022

The correct answer was the simplest one for the Warriors. The way to beat the Celtics was to follow the straightest, sharpest, steeliest line. If the Warriors were going to win Game 2 after kicking away Game 1, they had to harry, bump and bother the Celtics around once, twice or 50 times, if at all possible. Then bump and bother them again.

No tricks. No super-complicated defensive strategy. You guard that guy. You try to take the ball away. Straight line to the victory. Sometimes with Jaylen Brown, Jayson Tatum, Al Horford and the other Celtics standing in the way.

Pretty simple, right? Pretty ferocious, too.

"It was mostly physicality, intensity right from the beginning," Steve Kerr said of the Warriors' defensive focus in their 107-88 victory at Chase Center. "We only played one possession of zone the whole game. They made a 3, and we went away from that.

"I think it was important for us to stay in man-to-man in order to impose physicality on the game. You know, sometimes when you sit back in zone, it puts you on your heels a little bit. And we did a lot of that in Game 1. That was one adjustment. We didn't know how much zone we'd play coming in. But our man-to-man was really good, so we just stayed with it."

The leader in any Warriors defensive attack, of course, is always going to be Draymond Green, who was surprisingly muted during the Warriors' Game 1 loss and especially when Boston erupted for nine 3-pointers in an amazing fourth-quarter barrage. But that was when Green was mostly matched up with big man spot-up shooter Horford (who made 6 of 8 shots from long distance and scored 26 points in Game 1) or wandering around in the zone defense the Warriors have been playing quite frequently this postseason.

This time, Kerr switched Green onto the much more dynamic Brown for most of the game (after Green set the tone on the first play of the game by tying up Horford for a jump ball) and stayed in man-to-man — and there were ripple effects from there. That put Klay Thompson, less prone to wander from his man, on Horford, which perplexed the Celtics enough that Horford didn't even attempt a 3-pointer and scored only two points.

"They did a good job of staying with me, for example," Horford said of the problems the Warriors caused. "Obviously, I didn't get an attempt, not even a look. So they did a good job of making sure they took me away."

It also set loose Green against Brown in an entirely unsubtle and quite forceful way. Brown struggled to a 5-of-17 shooting night and was unhappy with a few of the bumps and wrestling matches Green pulled him into. Maybe Green could have been called for more fouls, but he wasn't. Maybe he could have been whistled for his second technical foul of the game (and ejected) when he fell alongside Brown in the second quarter and kept his legs on top of Brown's body for a beat or two longer than necessary and the two exchanged shoves. But there was no technical, and Green was not ejected.

He had his assignment. He did not get derailed from it.

"Draymond's way better when he's in the fray, guarding the ball, guarding the toughest assignments," Kerr said of the switch onto Brown. "He loves that. He embraces it. So I think it worked out better with him on Jaylen and sliding Klay over to Horford. It worked tonight, but you never know how this goes in Game 3."

The adjustment discombobulated the Celtics offense almost immediately, and it never got recombobulated. As Stephen Curry said after Game 1, which the Warriors lost 120-108: The Warriors scored plenty enough to win that game. The problem was the defense allowing too many open shots for the Celtics' secondary scorers. Guess what? The Warriors scored 107 in Game 2 and won going away.

In the third quarter, everything went haywire for the Celtics, who were outscored 34-15, giving the Warriors a 23-point lead going into the fourth quarter. Overall, Boston committed 18 turnovers and couldn't get its supporting players into the flow the way Horford, Marcus Smart and Derrick White lit up the Warriors in Game 1.

"I think everybody played with more force," Green said. "It wasn't just me on Jaylen Brown. It was across the board. If I just pick up my force and no one else does, it doesn't work. It's a total team effort, guys being ready to help when help is needed, and guys taking on the challenge at the point of attack.

"Yes, I wanted to come out and be more aggressive on that side, and I think I did a good job of that. But that's a full team effort. It doesn't just work because of one guy."

Curry, who was as good defensively in Game 2 as he was on offense (29 points, including an explosive 14 when the Warriors broke it open in the third quarter), had a slightly more direct conclusion when asked if putting Green on Brown changed the Warriors' intensity.

"You could've put Draymond on coach (Ime) Udoka and it would have been a different ballgame from (Game 1) just based on the way he approached the game," Curry said. "Matchups are matchups. But everybody has to bring the right intensity, and Draymond did that from the jump."

With Draymond leading the way, all the Warriors needed was one more push, which came when Gary Payton II, out since Game 2 of the second round when he fractured his left (shooting) elbow in Memphis, checked in halfway through the first period to a standing ovation. He went on to play 25 outstanding minutes, including several stints guarding Tatum.

Essentially, GP2, who nailed an open 3 and two layups, flipped roles with Jordan Poole in this game (he played six more minutes than Poole through the third quarter, when the game was still in doubt). There was a point to that. Again, the very simplest kind: The Warriors wanted to make this game as tough as possible for the Celtics offense. And they wanted to be tough.

"The physicality, the on-ball defense, Gary's special in that regard," Kerr said. "So all the change

in the way the game felt from an intensity standpoint, Gary had a huge role in that. He's getting into Tatum, into Brown, he's sprinting the floor in transition, he gives us extra speed, makes it easier for us to score in transition. He was fantastic."

Another adjustment was a surprise: Kerr put Nemanja Bjelica, who has been in and out of the postseason rotation, into the second unit alongside Poole, Thompson, Otto Porter Jr. and Andrew Wiggins. (Green was in that group in Game 1 but stayed on the floor with Curry longer in this game.) That unit was decent to start the second quarter, which meant that Kerr could hold back Curry a little bit instead of pushing toward the outer limits of his endurance.

Bjelica made a couple of baskets, grabbed a few rebounds and played very solid defense even when he was switched onto Tatum, and the second unit had lost only one point by the time Kerr got Curry back in at the 8:11 mark.

"He was good," Kerr said of Bjelica. "We wanted to give him some minutes. He was really good in the Memphis series and Dallas Game 5 when we played. He's been good every time we've put him out there. His defense is holding up really well, and he gives us playmaking and floor-spacing offensively, which you need against this team."

The Warriors' huge third quarter, coupled with avoiding a repeat of the Game 1 fourth-quarter collapse, also allowed Kerr to rest Curry for the entire fourth quarter and keep his playing time to just 32 minutes (when he probably was on pace to play 42 or more in this game if it had remained close).

That was good for the Warriors in the moment and even better for the long haul in this series, which shifts to Boston for Games 3 and 4.

"Anywhere we can find rest for him in this series is going to be important," Kerr said. "We got him four minutes in the second quarter and held up pretty well. I thought that was important. It's good to keep his minutes down."

This is going to be a long series. The Warriors are good. Boston is good. And the Warriors have no illusions that they figured everything out in Game 2. They did good things, they made some smart adjustments, and mostly they just played with the necessary force.

"It's 1-1 and we know it's going to get a lot harder," Kerr said. "I don't have any predictions or premonitions or anything about how the rest of the series goes. I just know we have to bring that level of intensity and physicality to beat Boston, because they're a hell of a team."

If there's one difference between these two teams, it's that the Warriors have proved over and over, from 2015 to now, that they can adjust their strategy and rev up the aggressiveness when they absolutely must. To beat them, you have to do it, too, and you have to do it better and more powerfully than they do. It's pretty simple. It's very difficult. ▬▬▬

'Swimming Upstream'

After Game 3 loss, Warriors Must Match Celtics' Hunger

By Marcus Thompson II

JUNE 9, 2022

Klay Thompson said he got 2015 vibes, given the Warriors' current predicament. After a 116-100 loss in Game 3, putting Boston two wins from a title, he tried to make a connection between this season's Celtics and those Cavaliers. He pointed to the isolation-heavy offense, the shooters all over who spread out the floor and the presence of an All-NBA superstar. But it wasn't long before he realized the comparison didn't land. So he settled on the only real connection between history and the present.

"Just being down 2-1 in a championship series," Thompson said, "like, we've been here before. We can rely on our experience."

As they were seven years ago, the Warriors are on the road. As they did in 2015, they now face a must-win Game 4 in a hostile environment. They have to figure out a way to conquer the Celtics.

"To Klay's point," Curry said, "it does help knowing that we've been through a little of everything the last eight years and can draw through that experience of when you need to, to stay in the series."

It makes sense why they would lean on this. The powers of positive thinking require a hunt for silver linings and hopeful omens. The truth, though: So much more is meaningfully different this time.

Primarily, the Warriors' stars are seven years older, with the scars to prove it. That was most evident in Draymond Green, who played "like shit." After calling himself out in Game 1, he was a menace in Game 2. But repeating that effort in Game 3 looked to be asking for a lot against a front line that has him beat in just about every category — bigger, stronger, faster, more explosive — save for experience.

Andre Iguodala's contributions are now mostly cerebral. Thompson, who finally found his shooting touch, has his hands full with Celtics wing Jaylen Brown and is not the defender he was back then.

Also, these Celtics are better — more athletic, more talented in their top seven or eight players, more physically challenging — than the Cavaliers of that year. In 2015, the Warriors knew they were the better team. Now, the question is do they have enough?

Something, however, can be taken from Golden State's inaugural title run in 2015. It's that the Warriors didn't have a championship when they pulled it off. Seven years ago, they didn't lean on experience. It was desperation that got them through. It was an urgency that pushed them over the top. That's what they will need again.

If anything, in these Celtics, they are facing themselves from 2015. If the Warriors win this series, it won't be because they've won a championship before. If they get a game in Boston, it won't be because they've won a road game in 26 straight series and thus a road victory is owed to them.

Through three games, it is clear the Warriors' experience is proving no match for the Celtics' hunger. The reassurance of past success isn't generating enough defiance. This season has been validation that Golden State's core still has championship DNA. It's proven it can compete for a championship. But this isn't a championship roster. Not yet, anyway. That's how the Warriors need to play: not to preserve their legacies but as if they are being forged by this series.

Wednesday was another slow start and discombobulated finish. The Celtics have been revved up to start games and, in the two fourth quarters that mattered, had another gear to close.

Are the Warriors hungry enough to compete on the boards? To remain focused? To execute? To match the energy of their foe? When they do, they win. But in Game 3?

"We were kind of plugging holes," Warriors coach Steve Kerr said. "They did a good job. They earned the win. They put a lot of pressure on us, and (we) felt like we were kind of swimming upstream most of the night."

The Warriors need to look no further than the second and third quarters of Game 3 to know they can beat the Celtics. The Warriors were on the brink of another road blowout as Boston did just

about everything right. But desperation kicked in, just as it did in Game 2 after their first home loss of the postseason.

Golden State had been blown out in Memphis and Dallas when the home team was cooking, trailing by as much as 55 at the Grizzlies and 29 at the Mavericks. But the exigencies of the clicking Celtics triggered the Warriors. Curry went into attack mode. Thompson, after a rough first stint, stopped forcing shots as if his reputation would guide them in. The Warriors scored 67 points in the middle quarters, erasing a 15-point first-quarter deficit and leaving the raucous Boston crowd shook. It felt like the Warriors were going to do their Warriors thing.

But the fourth quarter began, and the Celtics showed they weren't cowering to the mystique. Boston ramped up the pressure on Curry. And for the second time in this series, the Warriors played the final 12 minutes as if prestige would save them.

"(We) had some unforced turnovers the first couple possessions of the fourth," Curry said, "and that obviously led to them getting some easy buckets, extending the lead a little bit. We settled down a little bit after that and got some good shots. They tried to send a little more attention to our pick-and-rolls.

"I think we could slow down just a little bit and try to find the right matchups. But that first two or three minutes kind of set the tone for the rest of the fourth and gave them a little bit of a cushion. We had a hard time responding after that."

Curry turned it over three times in the first three minutes of the fourth, twice dumping it off in traffic, the third forcing the kind of long outlet pass that has not worked all series. The Celtics, meanwhile, spread it out, put the ball in Tatum's hands and patiently hunted for smart shots.

The Warriors turned it over six times in the first 10 minutes of the fourth quarter. Nine of their 16 shots in the quarter were from 3-point range.

"I thought I had a lot of open 3s I just didn't make," said Andrew Wiggins, who finished 1-of-6 from beyond the arc. "But just got to keep shooting, keep shooting with confidence and then they will drop."

That's another similarity to 2015. The crew around the Warriors' trio of stars are mostly veterans who are at a point where a championship changes the tenor of their career. In 2015, it was Iguodala, Andrew Bogut, Shaun Livingston, David Lee and Leandro Barbosa. The supporting cast had one youngster in Harrison Barnes. Iguodala won the NBA Finals MVP because he stepped up in support of Curry — which was vital because Thompson, who scored 34 in Game 2, totaled just 40 points over the final four games of the 2015 NBA Finals. Green turned it up, too, averaging 16.3 points in the final three games.

This year's supporting cast is made up of vets looking to change their stars with a title: Wiggins, Otto Porter Jr., Gary Payton II. The Harrison Barnes of this crew is Jordan Poole. They don't have the memories of 2015 to drive them. Yet they will largely determine this series.

The Celtics had three players with at least 24 points and five assists. Robert Williams III was a game-changing force. Al Horford plays like the hungriest man out there sometimes. Even Grant Williams was effective off the bench. The Warriors got 56 points from the Splash Brothers, but the Celtics got great games up and down the roster.

Perhaps that means Kerr, who's pressed the right buttons all playoffs, should lean into his team's hunger instead of waiting for the champions to find old form. Green didn't have it all night. He played soft, by his own admission. If he doesn't have the fire that night, maybe 35 minutes isn't the way to help him find it.

Also, maybe the Warriors shouldn't be above lobbying the refs on behalf of Curry. He took one free throw in Game 3, his fewest of the playoffs, and it was a product of Horford stepping into his landing space on a 3.

Curry's 38 drives in this series, per NBA Stats, are second only to Tatum's 43. It was Tatum's 19 drives in Game 3 that took the lead from Curry. But the Warriors star has only two free throws on those drives while Tatum has 10 on his. That disparity was underscored by Curry, whom the Celtics offense hunted, as he picked up two fouls early and had his fourth early in the third. Two of the fouls were well-earned. The other two were bad breaks as Curry didn't get away with the same handiness he gets defended with.

All Curry would say:

"It is hard to understand the flow of the game based on some of the calls that went my way where I have four and you're having to defend a certain way because you want to stay on the floor and not allow that to impact the game. But you know, you've still got to find a way to be effective no matter how the game's being called, and it's a good lesson to learn for the next game."

It's not Curry's style, or Kerr's, to lobby the refs publicly. But desperation seeks out whatever edge it can find. The Celtics sounded the alarm after Game 2 when Green was getting away with hacking. Considering the title hopes rest on Curry, and he could be hobbled in Game 4, maybe the Warriors put away decorum and eat whatever fine comes their way. Leave no stone unturned.

These Celtics are hungry. They smell blood. They are relentless. Past championships won't save the Warriors. Matching the Celtics' hunger is what it will take. ▬▬

'The Heart on That Man is Incredible'

Stephen Curry Stuns Boston with a Roar and a Historic Outing

By Marcus Thompson II

JUNE 11, 2022

It was a routine step-back 3-pointer, albeit his second in a row. It gave the Warriors a five-point lead. It came with 2:03 left in the first quarter. Nothing about this sequence, and when it occurred, suggested it was of special significance.

Still, after watching his swish, and after the Celtics called a timeout, Steph Curry had something to say. He walked away from the Warriors' bench, all the way to the other end of the court. Yelling. Flexing. Taunting. On the baseline near the Boston bench, he roared into the sea of green and white, as if he wanted to tremble their souls. They say a tiger's roar is strong enough to paralyze its prey. Curry usually saves his demonstrative displays for the big moments, when the opponent is vanquished. But this night, in the early stages of this must-win game for the Warriors, he wasn't celebrating a conquest. He was prepping it.

He pointed to the hallowed hardwood beneath his feet and declared the reality the Celtics are facing. They would have to deal with an all-time great this night. All night.

"He wasn't letting us lose," Draymond Green said.

That he did not. Curry scored 43 points on 14-for-26 shooting with 10 rebounds in a 107-97 win in Game 4. A Curry Classic on Causeway. He snatched home-court advantage from the clutches of the Celtics. Boston had a chance to take a commanding lead. But Curry flexed, and the Warriors head home for Game 5.

Curry's had some big NBA Finals games before, contrary to popular narratives. In 2015, he scored 17 of his 37 in the fourth quarter of a pivotal Game 5, going bucket-for-bucket with LeBron James to take control of the series. In 2016, Game 4 on the road in Cleveland, with the wear and tear of his sprained knee taking its toll, Curry scored 24 of his 38 in the second half to put the Warriors up 3-1 in the series. He totaled 47 points, eight rebounds and seven assists in Game 3 of the 2019 finals despite facing a box-and-one defense from the Raptors while Kevin Durant and Klay Thompson were sidelined with injuries. Two

games later, Curry finished with 31 points, eight rebounds and seven assists in a huge Game 5 win in Toronto to keep the Warriors alive.

But what happened this night in Boston was a performance that vaults his legend. He left even his harshest critics with frayed vocal cords. Beneath the 17 championship banners hanging in the rafters of TD Garden, on the parquet floor graced by legends like Kevin Garnett and Kobe Bryant, Curry showed the basketball world he is, indeed, him.

"The heart on that man is incredible," Thompson said.

Game 4 was the flashy exhibit often necessary for proper acclaim. It was the type of monster performance expected from players of his ilk. But this game was but another episode in his legacy of winning. Coming out on top so often commands a grittiness, requires a hero's resolve. His superpower is shooting, but his greatest strength is his will to win.

His 43-point night was born of one of his greatest attributes. Sure, it was a clinic of shooting and ballhandling, but such were secondary. The star was his indomitable will, a frame that belies his toughness. His resilience cannot be understated. His entire story is a case study in determination. This was just the latest example of his disregard for odds.

You want to know why the Warriors have now won a road game in 27 consecutive series? Wardell Stephen Curry II. With Game 4, the Warriors have won 39 road playoff road games in the Curry era. He's scored at least 30 points in 20 of them.

"I don't rank my performances," Curry said. "Just win the game."

Nothing reveals fortitude in the NBA like winning on the road. And Boston's intimidating venue requires a tenacious spirit. The Celtics fans had been cussin' out Green for two games. They shouted spicy speech at Thompson, too, after he called them "rude" and threw shade at their classiness. A retort was required. So the 6-foot-3 fella from Davidson played the role of big brother leading the Warriors through the proverbial alley, darkened by Celtics vitriol. He yelled back at them. And when the crowd started spewing pro-

fanity his way, he responded with big baskets and scoring spurts.

Remember, he did this two days after a 6-foot-9, 240-pound man fell on his left foot, setting off another injury watch as the world waited to see if he was hurt.

Curry can't stand when his health becomes the storyline, a complex born of his ankle troubles early in his years. But, in hindsight, his sore left foot tipped his hand. He was determined to play and not to talk about his foot. He wanted all doubt about Game 4 on Boston's side of the aisle.

"I could tell in his demeanor the last couple days," Green said, "even after Game 3, that he was going to come out with that type of fire."

Remember, the Celtics offense is hunting him. Curry can't hide and rest on defense.

He has been the defender on 52 Boston field goal attempts in this series, per NBA Stats. More than Marcus Smart and Jaylen Brown. Opponents are shooting 44.2 percent against Curry. After going 10-for-16 against foul-plagued Curry in Game 3, the Celtics were 4-for-11 when Curry defended in Game 4.

Remember, he did this against the No. 1 defense in the league — which is bigger and stronger at every position and plays with a physicality that breaches boundaries and breaks spirits.

Curry has seen just about every defense imaginable. He's been face-guarded the length of the court, doubled 40 feet from the basket, trapped and blitzed. But the Celtics pose unique problems. Their smallest player is the 2022 Defensive Player of The Year, and he plays like his freedom is on the line. Smart is so good at what he does, and so consistently abrasive, he gets away with a lot of otherwise illegal contact. The entire Boston defense has picked up on that game plan — get into Curry, do whatever it takes to stay connected, even if that means holding when he's off the ball and hand-checking when he's on it. Plus, the Celtics have the advantage on Curry in girth, athleticism, strength and length. Yet he battles through it, like he would've had to if he'd played in his father's day.

And look what he's doing against this Celtics' defense in this series: averaging 34.3 points on 50 percent shooting, including 25-of-51 from 3.

"Just stunning," Steve Kerr said. "The physicality out there is, you know, pretty dramatic. I mean, Boston's got obviously the best defense in the league. Huge and powerful at every position. And for Steph to take that — that kind of pressure all game long and still be able to defend at the other end when they are coming at him shows you, I think, this is the strongest physically he's ever been in his career, and it's allowing him to do what he's doing."

Another big third quarter, his favorite, put the Warriors in position to come out of New England with renewed life.

He came off a screen going to his right and drilled a three over Derrick White from the right wing, cutting the Celtics' lead to three. He came off another screen going left, firing before Robert Williams III could react and before White could recover. The Celtics' lead was down to one. Going left off a Gary Payton II screen, he pulled up from 33 feet, suddenly enough for Jayson Tatum to run into the back of him. That one tied the game. Then, in a play that gets added to the highlight reel, he drove and dished to the corner, then relocated to that same corner, splashing another 3 to put the Warriors ahead by a point.

"We were there," Smart said. "He made a lot of the shots where we were contesting from behind. We had somebody there and he was just making them. That's what he does."

This put Kerr in a tough spot. Curry was at 31 minutes, 28 seconds at the start of the fourth quarter. He normally sits for the first six minutes of the quarter. That's been cut to about four minutes in the playoffs. Last game, Kerr had to cut it to just over two. That's because the Celtics have dominated the fourth quarters. In Game 1, they owned it 40-16. In Game 3, it was 23-11.

Curry was rolling, and the Warriors needed offense to stave off a pending Celtics rally. But Kerr stuck with his gut. He doesn't like Curry over 40 minutes. There are diminishing returns. While the threat Curry is on the court is helpful, Kerr's expertise on his superstar knows he is better with even a short rest. So he opened the fourth with Curry on the bench.

"He was not happy," Kerr said. "I felt pretty good about where we were. The other night he played the whole fourth, and I didn't love the way that quarter went, not because of how he played, but I think we were in a pretty good spot. You know, to buy him a few minutes in that fourth quarter to start, I think to me was important. But you never know how it all plays out. You just kind of go with your gut."

The move didn't doom the Warriors. Boston led by as many as five, but that only set up the cap to Curry's historic night. The ball was in his hands. The Celtics defense was scattered. His presence put pressure on their offense to score. It all colluded to break Boston.

The Celtics led by two when Curry pushed it in transition. He drew three defenders, which left Thompson open for a 3 at the top. The Warriors took the lead for good. The next time down, Curry eluded Smart on a screen and danced with Williams on the perimeter. A series of crossovers led to an easy 12-foot floater.

Then with just inside of two minutes left, Green led a fast break. He got stopped at about the free throw line. But he knew exactly where to go. All the attention was on him, as he had the ball. It was enough for Curry to get free from White for a split second. He stepped into a Green bounce pass, gave a little jab and ratted home the dagger 3.

Then, after the Celtics called a timeout, their hopes crushed and facing the reality of a long series, it was finally time to celebrate the conquest. He flexed. He pounded his chest. He taunted. Curry waded into the mystique of the Celtics — as did Kobe before him, and Magic Johnson, and Dr. J — and made the kind of statement legends make. He is him. ▬▬▬

Strength in Numbers

Curry's Teammates Step Up to Edge Closer to Title

By Sam Amick

JUNE 14, 2022

When it comes to basketball body language, Steph Curry has always been pretty easy to read. You get the moments like early in his Game 4 masterpiece in Boston, when he flexed as if he were on the cover of Men's Health after a first-quarter 3-pointer and shouted at the Celtics fans who had been dropping f-bombs on his most beloved teammates. Translation: "Here I come..."

But then there are the times like late in the fourth quarter of Game 5 of the NBA Finals at Chase Center, when Curry misfired on a 3-pointer for the ninth time in nine tries, but Gary Payton II corralled the ball for a putback layup and a 16-point Warriors lead with 1:19 to go. Curry, his arms spread wide in exasperation and his head angled toward the sky as if he were some poor sap who was stuck on the side of the road with a flat tire, turned back toward Payton and gave him a hearty hug. Translation: "Strength in Numbers is a beautiful thing."

Or something like that.

After four finals games of Curry at his best, with everyone from Klay Thompson to Draymond Green and others saying that the other Warriors had to pitch in a whole lot more after he'd carried them for so long, this was the kind of group effort that defined those pre-Kevin Durant teams that lived by that corny-but-true motto. Even with Curry shooting as if he couldn't have hit water if he fell out of Thompson's beloved boat, missing 15 of 22 shots overall and (no typo here) going a historic 0-for-9 from 3, the Warriors head to Boston with a 3-2 series lead. Their 104-94 Game 5 victory was born out of his dominance.

All that unmatched gravity Curry creates, and the defensive fear that comes with it, finally led to the game they all were sure was coming before this was all over. And the fact that some of the OGs from the "Strength in Numbers" days are wearing suits to the games now instead of jerseys — namely Warriors executives Shaun Livingston and Zaza Pachulia — says everything about the persistence of the culture they all created years ago.

"Just the strength in numbers," Payton said. "We have a bunch of guys that are ready at all times. And you know when their number is called, they come in and give us a good push, good energy, good vibe on the court. Could be for 30 seconds, two minutes. You know, whoever comes in, steps up. They come in and do their job and keep the same focus that we had."

Andrew Wiggins, whose metamorphosis from his Minnesota days to this is one of the most unexpected NBA stories in recent years, had the game of his life (26 points, 13 rebounds, Jayson Tatum defensive duty throughout). Thompson, he of the devastating injuries and age-of-enlightenment return, hit big shots when it mattered most (21 points) while playing his part in the Warriors' strong defensive effort (18 Celtics turnovers, 41.3 percent shooting).

Payton — the 29-year-old whose career was on the brink last summer, and who fought his way back from that shoulder injury in early May against Memphis — picked the perfect time to shine, too (15 points on 6-of-8 shooting, five rebounds and three steals). Green, just three days removed from the brief benching late in Game 4 that tested his trust in coach Steve Kerr and marked the peak of his well-chronicled struggles in this series, set the early tone defensively and made his mark on both ends (eight points, six assists, eight rebounds and a plus-11 mark in 35 minutes). Jordan Poole, the third-year guard who has been as much of a wildcard in this matchup as anyone, added 14 points in 14 minutes (including another ridiculous 3 at the end of the third quarter, just like he had in Game 2).

Now here comes the bad part for the Celtics, who looked so ready to seize this championship moment in Game 3, only to drop two consecutive games for the first time this postseason (and for just the second time since mid-January). Curry, who loves golf nearly as much as he does basketball, just used his mulligan. The odds of him being this bad again are as likely as the notion of Celtics fans chanting their love for Green when he returns to TD Garden for Game 6.

"Obviously, we have spoke about helping him, and I don't think he's been out there helpless, like that's the narrative," Green explained. "But everybody's doing their part, and tonight, a night that he didn't have it going, we found offense elsewhere, and that's kind of what it's been.

"It was huge. Now, that's good for us. He was 0-for-9 from 3. He's going to be livid going into Game 6, and that's exactly what we need."

"I just know he'll respond," Thompson, who shot 34.2 percent from 3 in the first four games but hit 5 of 11 3s in Game 5, said of Curry. "He's one of the greatest competitors I've ever been around. And he's a perfectionist, like myself. I know he'll be thinking about the shots he missed. And that's a good thing, because Thursday, hopefully, most of the time, he regresses to the mean. And it's scary when he does."

Great players have bad games in the finals. It's just a fact. The most memorable example I've witnessed in person came in 2010, when the late, great Kobe Bryant shot 6-of-24 in Game 7 against Boston.

Bryant still won the Finals MVP award, and rightfully so. And if these Warriors finish the job, Curry's Game 5 stinker will be excusable in the same kind of way. His team wouldn't be here without him, but his teammates sure do revel in those nights when they can return the favor.

"I don't think I've ever been happier after a 0-for-whatever type of night, just knowing the context of the game, the other ways you tried to impact the game and the fact that, you know, you had four guys step up in meaningful ways to help us win offensively," Curry said. "So all that stuff matters. Yeah, there's a fire burning, and I want to make shots, but the rest of it is about how we win the game, and we did that." ■■■■

Championship DNA

Warriors Win Fourth Title in Eight Seasons, Curry Named Finals MVP

By Joe Vardon

JUNE 17, 2022

The scene was so familiar, Stephen Curry wrapped in Steve Kerr's embrace. Or Klay Thompson in Draymond Green's. Or mix and match.

In just two seasons, the Golden State Warriors went from worst back to first. It was as though they never left. The dynasty reigns on, and the Warriors are again NBA champions after conquering the Boston Celtics in six games with a 103-90 victory in Game 6.

"They are all unique, they are all special," Kerr said. "I think this one may have been the most unlikely, just from the standpoint of where we've been the last couple years."

The victory over Boston makes four titles in eight seasons for the team coached by Kerr, piloted by Curry, with Thompson as his wingman and Green as the backbone, and it fell on the same date, June 16, as the night these Warriors won their first title together — seven years ago in Cleveland.

Two seasons ago, with Kevin Durant gone, Thompson on the shelf with a torn knee ligament, and Curry out for most of the season with a broken hand, the Warriors lost 50 games — the most in the NBA during a pandemic-shortened campaign.

"I can say it now: I don't know how many teams could carry that as long as we have with the expectations of comparing us now to teams of (the) past and make it to the mountaintop again," Curry said.

As expected, Curry shook off a historically poor shooting performance from Game 5 to pace the victors with 34 points on six 3s. He added seven rebounds and seven assists, and, in a departure from the norm, was named NBA Finals Most Valuable Player for the first time.

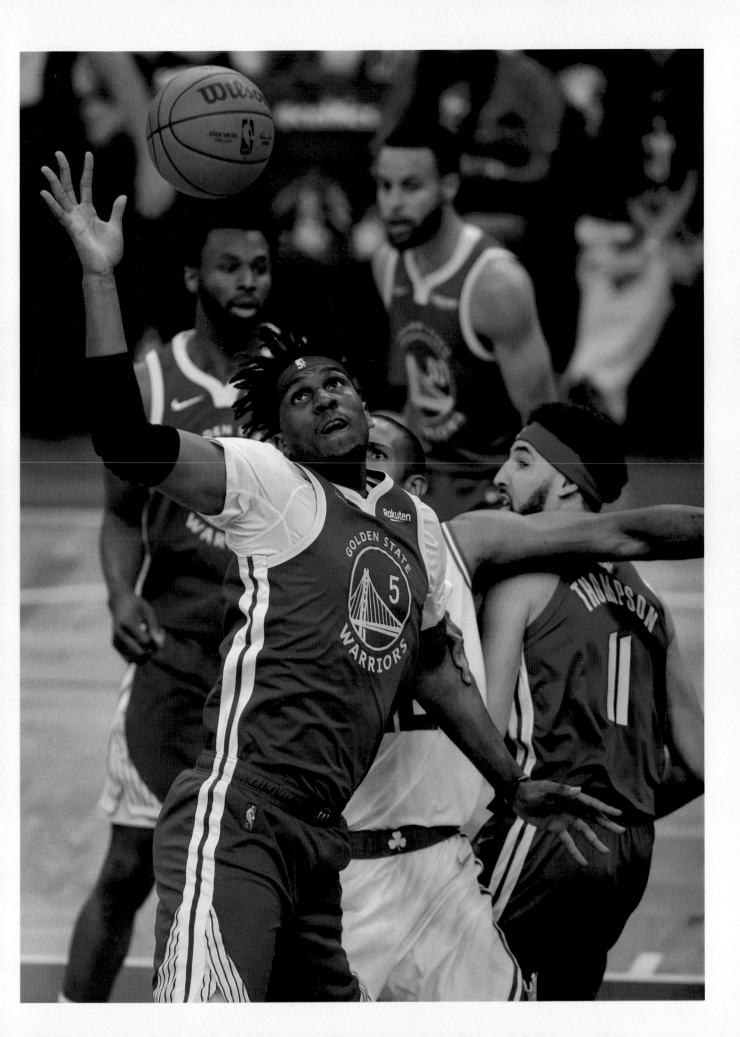

In six mostly brilliant games in these finals, Curry averaged 31.2 points and shot 44.2 percent from 3-point range. He fell one 3-pointer shy of tying his own finals record for 3s in a series (32), but he somehow shot 0-of-9 in Game 5, ending two of his record streaks: one for consecutive games with at least one 3 in postseason games and another for most games in a row with a 3, regular or postseason.

Thompson, who is known this time of year as "Game 6 Klay," added 12 points, five rebounds and two 3s. He returned to action in January after more than two years away from the sport, due to two devastating leg injuries. By comparison to past Game 6s, this one was hardly memorable — statistically — for him. But it was the end of an arduous, trying journey back to the court.

"I saw it in the beginning of (the) season. People called me crazy," Thompson said. "I said 'championship or bust,' because I saw how we came out of the gate, 18-2. And playing just that Warriors brand of basketball that made us so successful, and then knowing I was going to be inserted in that, I knew we had a chance to do something special, and here we are. It's so incredible. Wow."

Green, maligned at times during the finals for poor offensive play and for picking on the Celtics, was sensational with 12 points, 12 rebounds, and eight assists. The newcomers to the dynasty, Andrew Wiggins and Jordan Poole, finished with 18 and 15 points, respectively.

Curry, Thompson and Green have now won 21 finals games together — the most of any trio in the past 50 years. Andre Iguodala was also a part of all four championship teams, including this one, but didn't play until the final minute in Boston.

"Me, Dray, Klay and Andre, we finally got that bad boy," Curry said. "It's special. It's special. Just all the work that went into it, the faith and belief and everybody in that locker room that's getting to spray champagne around the locker room, everybody mattered in that process. So I'm just proud of everybody."

This is the Warriors' seventh title overall, dating to 1947 when they played in Philadelphia. They trail only the Celtics and the Lakers for the most titles in league history, at 17 apiece. They are just the second opposing team in history to close out a finals in Boston and the first since the Los Angeles Lakers did it in 1985.

The Celtics, who were in 11th place in the East in mid-January before surging in the second half of the season, were playing with a first-time coach and with a drastic shift away from a traditional point guard, which had allowed them to bludgeon teams for months with a stingy defense. It worked all the way through Game 3 of the finals, after which they held a 2-1 lead.

From that point on, they couldn't stop Curry or hang on to the ball, and when Curry went cold in Game 5, the rest of the Warriors made Boston pay for leaving them open.

"It's going to hurt. It will hurt for a while," Celtics coach Ime Udoka said. "Probably that stuff never goes away. That was part of the message: Let it propel us forward, the experience, (the) growth and progress that we made this season. Obviously, getting to your ultimate goal and (falling) a few games short is going to hurt. There are a lot of guys in there (who are) very emotional right now."

The Celtics lost the last three games of the finals, marking the first time since Dec. 25-29 that they'd dropped three in a row, and they committed at least 15 turnovers in each of the three losses. On Thursday, Boston gave the ball away a season-worst 22 times and fell to 0-8 this postseason when it hit that 15-turnover threshold.

Jaylen Brown, who finished with 32 points on Thursday, led the Celtics in scoring for the game and the series. Al Horford added 19 points, and Jayson Tatum struggled, finishing with 13 points on 6-of-18 shooting. The Warriors bench dominated the Celtics reserves once again, outscored them 21-5.

"Offensively, we were not good this series," Brown said. "Give credit to the Warriors. They forced us into doing stuff that we didn't want to do, and that resulted in turnovers, et cetera. At times, we just got to be better. That's it."

The Celtics opened play in Game 6 with the appropriate edge and desperation. They led 14-2 in the first quarter, and the TD Garden crowd, tense as it filed into the arena, erupted in relief and eu-

phoria. There would be more times to cheer, another point when it even felt like the Celtics might be in the game again. But it was a mirage.

Golden State went on a 35-8 run from 7:48 of the opening period well into the second. The Warriors led by 22 with 6:12 left in the third quarter after a Curry 3, and as the Celtics called timeout, Curry pointed to his ring finger in celebration.

The Celtics got back in the game behind 10 points from Brown and 12 from Horford to end the quarter, perhaps offering the last glimmer of hope.

Curry's 3-pointer with 3:17 to go put the Warriors ahead 96-81 and erased any lingering doubt. It was the fitting end to a finals where there was never a doubt as to the best player, the leader, the transcendent figure. As the final seconds ticked off the clock, Curry fell into embrace with his father, Dell, and then turned to the court with his head in his hands.

"I blacked out for a second," Curry said. "These last two months of the playoffs, these last three years, this last 48 hours, every bit of it has been an emotional roller coaster on and off the floor, and you're carrying all of that on a daily basis to try to realize a dream and a goal like we did tonight."

In 2015, while LeBron James dominated, Iguodala was named MVP for slowing him down. In 2017 and 2018, the award and the series belonged to Durant. The loss to the Raptors in the 2019 finals, during which Durant and Thompson suffered injuries, the bottoming out in 2020 and a failure to make the playoffs followed.

But this season, after the Warriors' strong start, Thompson eventually returned. Green looked more like his former self. And the newer players like Poole, Wiggins and Gary Payton II began to find their niches in the Warriors' machine.

They beat Denver in five games. Memphis in six. Dallas in five. They lost the series opener to Boston and trailed again after Game 3. When they turned it around this time, it was Curry at center stage, like he has been throughout the Warriors dynasty, just not at this particular point in the journey — with the confetti falling, the cigars lit and the Warriors hoisting trophies.

"I'm obviously thrilled for everyone in that room, and a lot of people had a big hand in this, but I think the thing with Steph is, you know, without him, none of this happens," Kerr said. "That's not taking anything away from Joe (Lacob) and (Peter Guber's) ownership, because they have built an incredible organization. Bob Myers, hell of a GM. Our players, we have had so many great players, but Steph ultimately is why this run has happened." ▬▬

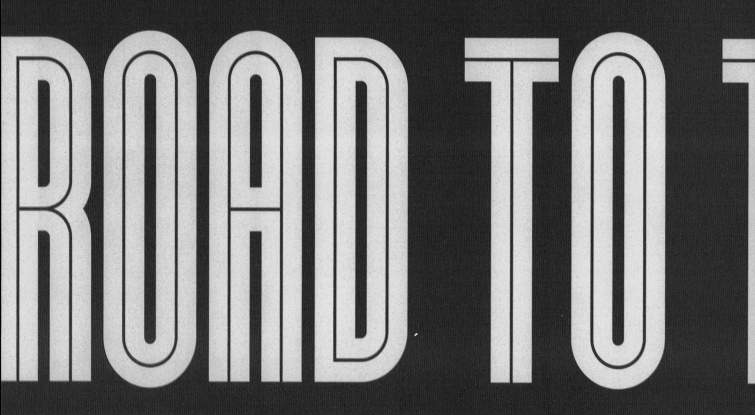

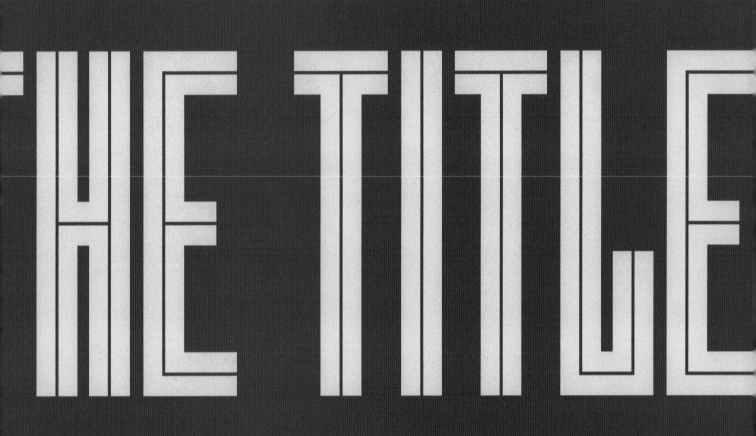

Stephen Curry

A Mere Mortal in Stature Who Slays Giants from a Distance

By Marcus Thompson II

JANUARY 31, 2022

If the psycho has to have a birthday, it was April 28, 2013.

Or maybe the birth happened before and this was his coming of age. Nonetheless, the timeline of this NBA lore starts here. In Oakland. Against Denver. In the first round of the playoffs.

In the third quarter, with a four-point Warriors lead, Jarrett Jack ran a pick-and-pop with Carl Landry. Jack dribbled around a screen to the right wing and bounced a pass back to Landry at the top of the key. Corey Brewer, the Nuggets' defense-oriented wing, scrambled to cover the open Landry. In doing so, he left Stephen Curry wide open.

Then suddenly, inconspicuously, the game clock froze. It was stuck on 6 minutes, 27 seconds. As if Brewer's decision created a warp in the basketball universe. As if time itself wanted to pause and witness what was about to happen.

Landry whipped a pass to Curry, who caught it and gave a pump fake to charging Denver forward Wilson Chandler. With the defender in the air, Curry stepped to his left, like he was avoiding a puddle, to reposition himself in open space of the left corner. Then he jacked up a 3 right in front of the Nuggets' bench.

"It was the magnitude of the moment," Curry said. "First playoff series. Unreal atmosphere. We were making a third-quarter run. I don't know what it was about that moment. Just, I was feeling it. I could feel everybody behind me. I don't know. It was like the perfect storm. Feeling their presence, the rhythm of the shot. Everything felt perfect. And I did it."

That he did. With his shot still ascending toward its apex, Curry debuted his signature flex. He turned 180 degrees. When the ball splashed through the net, Curry was facing the suddenly silenced Nuggets bench, his back to the very basket at which he aimed.

Even now, nearly nine years later, he doesn't know why he did it. Something just moved him. He can't even remember what was said, just that he heard the voice of JaVale McGee and felt the shadow of the Nuggets' animosity breathing down his neck. He can't articulate why this was his retort.

Perhaps that something was the psycho inside, the alter ego that helped produce a storybook career.

The idea of a legend has lost some of its luster in modernity. Not because greatness is less prominent but because little is left to the imagination. Everything is recorded, preserved for consumption, observable. But legends, real legends, are born of scarce witnesses. They survive through storytelling. They grow as time spreads its wingspan between the moment and the oration.

But feelings are difficult to behold through modern mediums. The emotion of experience doesn't always translate through highlights, leaving lore with a job to do.

His accomplishments are wholly impressive. Three-time NBA champion. Two-time MVP, one of 12 players to win back-to-back MVPs (2015, '16), including first unanimous selection in '16, when he led the league in points (30.1), steals (2.1) and free-throw percentage (.908). Only Rick Barry has led the league in all three categories and never in the same season.

The preeminent and premier 3-point shooter, who sets a new record every time he makes one. As of this writing, he has 3,050 made 3s, already 77 ahead of Ray Allen, the previous record holder, and 506 made 3s ahead of the next active player on the all-time list: James Harden. At .907, Curry is the career leader in free-throw percentage, as well. It should be no surprise that he's among the top 10 in career true shooting percentage at 62.3 percent, sixth-best in league history. He's also the only one under 6 foot 5.

He's the catalyst for the resurrection of an NBA franchise to greatness. According to StatMuse, Curry is seventh all-time in plus-minus: plus-5,361 in 808, the fewest amount of games in the top 15. He averages plus-6.6. Duncan, the all-time leader, averaged 6.4; LeBron averages 5.3. Simply, when Curry is on the court, the Warriors are winning. Five consecutive NBA Finals and three titles prove it.

But he holds an even more rare space because he is truly legendary, in the traditional sense. His game has an element best captured by the awe of the storyteller.

"I love Steph so much," Allen Iverson once said on Complex Sports' Load Management podcast. "That's why I made him my point guard. I think he changed the game sort of like I did. Greatest shooter that will ever play the game — that's what I think. The greatest basketball player I've seen with a jumper and handles like that. I'm just a big Steph Curry fan."

Wilt Chamberlain left people speechless as a mobile giant. Kareem Abdul-Jabbar astonished with a trick shot that never missed. Michael Jordan, and Dr. J before him, took everyone's breath away by walking on air, and Magic Johnson mesmerized with passes suggesting he had another set of eyes somewhere on his head. Their special greatness, the hold they had on viewers, extends beyond the data explaining their worth.

Curry is of their ilk. A mere mortal in stature who slays giants from a distance. And the trademark of his greatness, the autograph authenticating his legend, is his look-away 3. Nothing trumpets his unique brilliance like being so sure a long-distance shot is going in that he doesn't even see it

go in. He stamps his mastery of basketball's most pivotal act by declaring the absence of doubt when he shoots.

"He's incredibly arrogant on the floor and humble off the court," Warriors coach Steve Kerr said. "I think that's a really powerful combination."

This is the psycho's work. Not the meek fella who shocks people with his down-to-earthiness. Not the joyous kid who bubbles to the surface when he plays. Not the appreciative second-generation player anchored by his respect for the privilege and the fraternity.

When Curry jacks a 3-pointer and turns his back on the result, it's a wink from the maniac who lives inside his humble spirit.

"I know my favorite ones," Curry said. "I did it on Khris Middleton at home."

"I did it against Phoenix at home."

"Against Minnesota in China. Preseason."

Then there was that time in the 2016 Western Conference finals. He didn't just look away, but he turned his attention to then-Oklahoma City big man Serge Ibaka.

"Oh, in the playoffs," Curry said. "That was a nice one."

Make no mistake about it. Curry has reached such elevation, forced his way among the greats of all time because he's a merciless and relentless competitor. More than that, he is a savage who takes pleasure in destruction.

Such a personality was crafted out of necessity. Being smaller and overlooked all of his basketball life created the drive that got him here. Because of his slightness, because of the low expectations, his validation had to be that much more emphatic. Something Curry learned very early on was to vanquish doubt. He couldn't just put up a good case for himself. He had to make questioning him a ridiculous notion.

He didn't want to be a good 3-point shooter, he wanted to be the greatest. He didn't want to be just a shooter, he wanted to be a monster. He didn't want to win, he wanted to collect rings. And he doesn't want to just make plays, he wants to dance on graves.

The greatest ones have such a streak in them. That deep conviction that fuels their work ethic, that makes them want the biggest stage. Take it from one of the all-time psychos in Kobe Bryant.

"I see a calmness about him," Bryant once said about Curry. "I see a calmness about him. And I think it's something that a lot of players don't understand. So I think it's very hard for the fans to understand what I'm saying. Because most players don't get it. But there's a serious calmness about him, which is extremely deadly. Because he's not up. He's not down. He's not contemplating what just happened before or worrying about what's to come next. He's just there.

"And when a player has the skills, when he's trained himself to have the skills to be able to shoot, dribble left, right, etc., and then you mix that with his calmness and poise, and you have a serious, serious problem on your hands."

Initially, it was hard to spot beyond the infectious smile, the positive vibes and the familial persona that have come to be his brand. But his teammates, his opponents know it's there. His ardent followers love it about him.

It takes some maniac tendencies to shoot from 30 feet with such supreme confidence. It takes the supremest of confidence to lead a revolution against an entire construct, against tradition, against preconceived notions about a 6-foot-3 point guard with a baby face and his father's craft.

To become a legend, a real legend requires first being audacious.

In 20 years, Curry will be talked about with excitement reserved for the most legendary. Like the elders of today talk about Abdul-Jabbar and Bill Russell, and how their children revere Larry Bird and Charles Barkley. The technologically literate future will have all the advanced metrics at their disposal to see.

But they won't convey the insanity of how Curry in his prime shot it from so far and so accurately. How he was so terrifying that the geometry of the game changed, a generation started to follow him like disciples, and defenses devoted all their resources toward stopping him.

They will tell of the psycho who just stepped back farther, shot it more often, made even more 3s. And, as the legend will go, he didn't even have to look. ▬

One Word: Accountability

Inside the Construction of
the Warriors Defense

By Anthony Slater

NOVEMBER 23, 2021

T he late third quarter Jordan Poole dunk put the Golden State Warriors up 21 in Brooklyn. If ever there was an early season time to boast, this was it. Stephen Curry had been latched to the bench in foul trouble for several minutes, yet the non-Curry Warriors had blown the game open against Kevin Durant and James Harden. Poole's hammer was the punctuation point on a statement win.

He didn't celebrate too long. Poole landed, roared in the crowd's direction and then quickly pivoted and sprinted back upcourt, trying to catch up to DeAndre' Bembry, his man, who started the possession several strides ahead. Initial job well done. That's the type of get-back-in-the-mix transition hustle the Warriors have been demanding.

But defense is about more than effort and ability. Brains matter. You can try like hell but still commit destructive mental errors. Poole did here. He finally caught up to Bembry in the paint, as he was attempting to Euro step around Draymond Green for a layup. Bembry is a bench player averaging 4.7 points per game. Green, as Kerr asserted recently, is "the best defensive player in the world." Poole is best letting Green put out the unthreatening fire. Instead, he speeds up and hacks Bembry from behind.

Here's the sequence, which is very relevant to the larger picture on how, through 20 percent of the season, the Warriors somehow have the best statistical defense the league has seen since the 2016 Spurs.

Green could've let the mistake go. In the past two seasons, he probably would have. The championship expectations had vanished, dragging the daily demand for excellence out the door. But it's all back now. So even though it's mid-November and the 11-2 Warriors are up 21 on a title contender, Green screams in Poole's direction after the whistle.

"I'm right here!" he said.

Green wasn't alone. Steve Kerr jumped off the bench to get on his third-year guard.

"Draymond and I were both yelling at him," Kerr relayed a few days later. "Jordan was like: 'It's OK. It's OK.'"

Green's response?

"Draymond goes: 'It's not OK. It's your fourth foul. Steph already has four. I'm right here!'" Kerr said. "There were so many reasons not to foul."

Which is the main point from the veterans who have lived the NBA's playoff gauntlet. A small mistake can cost you a game. A game can cost you a title. The habits built in the months leading up help you avoid those marginal but fatal slips.

"Even if it was the first play of the game and we had no foul trouble, Draymond's there," Kerr said. "The whole point of defense is to lower the percentage chance of someone making it. Then every time you foul, they get two free throws — the points per possession are high on that — the opposing defense gets set, you're one step closer to the bonus."

The Warriors drafted two teenagers and added Otto Porter Jr., Nemanja Bjelica and Andre Iguodala to the mix this summer. That's two stiff shooters who have never been known as defenders and the second oldest player in the league. Their roster reconstruction prioritized the future (Jonathan Kuminga over Davion Mitchell), offensive spacing and passing. The fifth-ranked defense a season ago, many internally believed (including Green), had been sacrificed in the process.

But the 15-2 Warriors currently have a better defensive rating (100.0) than they've ever had in the Kerr era. Their previous best — 100.4, way back in Kerr's inaugural season, 2014-15 — ranked first in the NBA back then. Currently, in a league that's exploded in offensive potency during the last half-decade, they've been even stingier.

How?

A ton of factors. Too many to detail fully. But I spent the recent road trip asking around, attempting to get an answer on the main factors. One word kept surfacing: accountability. The Warriors have created a healthy environment of accountability at all three levels, from the youth to the veterans to the coaching staff, each aiding the other in the pursuit to limit points.

Accountability from the youth

As a rookie, Poole was a bad player on the league's worst team. In his second season, he didn't earn a rotation spot until March. He hasn't been on this stage long and has had little to puff his chest out about. So that transition dunk, in Brooklyn and on TNT, must've felt like a proud warning to all basketball viewers. He's here. He matters. He would probably like to soak in the moment.

But not even 15 seconds later, after hustling back and committing a minor error that certainly wouldn't cost the Warriors the win, an irate Green and his ticked-off coach were hurling critiques in his direction, not hiding their anger from the audience. There are those who wish Green would save the lesson for film the next day or a quiet moment on the bench, but it's Green. They know how he operates and the collateral damage that comes with a fully engaged version.

But how does Poole feel? This is the first season he's experienced that full wrath.

"It's really just coaching," Poole said. "That's all it is. Everybody has a different style. Some people are laid back, want to bring you to the side and casually talk to you. Others are loud and want to jump in your face and scream and get their point across. All you gotta do is take what the main piece is out of it, fix it and keep pushing. I was trying to get back in the play, Draymond had him, I fouled. It happens. He said whatever he said. We keep it pushing."

That answer came two days after the fact. What does Poole feel in the moment? Is it an eye-roll? Does he find it funny?

"That he doing all the screaming?" Poole said. "For sure, bro. For sure. He doing all the screaming and yelling and, it's like, I would've listened to you if you whispered it. You know what I'm saying? But that's who he is as a person. The energy gets going, the emotions are up during the game, you just take it with a grain of salt. You can't sulk or get in your feelings. He's essentially just teaching and everyone is a different kind of teacher."

Organizationally, because of owner Joe Lacob's sustainability vision, the Warriors have welcomed an ambitious challenge. They're trying to fuse two eras together, attempting to win while developing their next wave of talent, creating a sturdy enough bridge so the winning never stops. That means throwing NBA babies into the cauldron and relying on them to handle it well.

If they don't, the entire plan can splinter. But Poole says he's bulletproof. Jonathan Kuminga has earned an increased role because he's defending with desire and verve. Moses Moody has a mature game and seems to live, breathe and study anything Andre Iguodala says or does. Nobody behind the scenes has any complaints about James Wiseman's coachability.

Accountability from the veterans

All those Draymond Green demands don't land as well if he's halfway interested in the season. As he admitted Sunday night — read Marcus Thompson's piece here — he'd lost some of that love for the game the past two seasons. It's back now. His lifestyle choices have improved and he's in great shape, which allows him to fly around the court.

That matters for two reasons. The first is obvious. When at his physical best, he's as destructive a defensive force as the league has seen in a long time — in its history, he'd proudly argue. He wins isolation matchups, breaks up 2-on-1s, knows your scheme better than you do and is a menace on the weak side. He's the defensive engine and attitude and, currently, he looks like his prime self.

"I fuck up opposing offenses," he loves to say.

The second is a bit more subtle. It's about the way that can all permeate down a roster. It's much easier for Green to command full defensive effort if his teammates know he's giving it himself. Team defense, also, is about trust. It can be difficult for players to rotate over if they don't believe a teammate will help the helper.

But it didn't take long for veterans like Bjelica and Porter to realize that, in contrast with some of their past stops, Green is flying over to erase a mistake, Iguodala never screws up a rotation, Kevon Looney is willing to do the dirty work and even the franchise face, Steph Curry, has built himself into an attentive, sturdy, above-average perimeter and team defender, despite his global status and offensive workload. If everything around you is in rhythm, it's easier to be in rhythm.

"If there's a blow-by, we always have help side," Bjelica said. "We know how to react. You always feel, when you are weakside, if you trap the box, help will come."

And everyone rebounds. The Warriors are currently the third-best rebounding team in the league despite a constant size disparity and no league leaders in the category.

"If you watch tape, Andre Iguodala boxes out every single possession," Kerr said. "Otto Porter boxes out every single possession. Beli does a good job. Damion Lee. I just think we have a veteran group who understands if you plug all the leaks, you can keep that shell tight defensively and don't worry about who is going to get the rebound. You can do it as a team, collectively."

The personalities also seem to play off each other well. If everyone acted like Draymond, there'd probably be two weekly brawls. But they've added the right amount of temperature coolers.

"I do love the mix," Kerr said. "You have internal leaders like Bjelica and Otto who have been around, understand everything and they can kind of quietly share thoughts on the bench as the game is going on. Then you have Draymond ripping into guys. Then you have Steph putting his arm around them. Andre's making a cryptic comment. It's great. It just feels like the hierarchy is in a good place."

Accountability from the coaching staff

The Warriors overhauled their coaching staff this summer while Kerr and Green were preparing and competing in the Olympics. Last season's defensive coordinator, Jarron Collins, departed. Kenny Atkinson filled his spot on the front of the bench. But Atkinson arrived, in part, to help reform a struggling offense.

"Draymond asked me this summer, while we were in Tokyo, when I told him about the changes: 'Who's running the defense?'" Kerr said.

Mike Brown. Draymond liked the answer.

"That's good," he told Kerr. "Because every time I talk to Mike about defense the last couple years, his head would start to sweat."

That comment from Tokyo was relayed to Draymond during the road trip.

"It does start sweating, man," Green laughed. "He loves it. When you love it — even last year, when he'd explain a defensive drill or get involved, he'd start sweating and going crazy. I'd laugh at him and he'd say: 'Draymond, I love this shit, man! I'm excited!' One thing we've known in his career, he's always been a great defensive coach."

Brown focused primarily on offense the past couple seasons, which, in retrospect, seems like a curious choice. He's known as a defensive tactician who, in his head coaching days back in Cleveland, built some great team defenses around LeBron James despite odd-fitting personnel. That side of the ball is his specialty.

"We've had great defensive coaches," Kerr said. "Ron Adams. Ron mentored Jarron Collins. Jarron was tremendous last year. Fifth-ranked defense. But some of the changes we made over the summer were more about getting a different energy in the building."

Some in the louder portion of the Warriors' online fan base have started referring to Kerr as Steve 2.0 this season because of all the strategic changes he has made. Kerr said he didn't know that label existed. He's no longer on Twitter. He had to download it on his phone the other day to post a video in support of Julius Jones, but then immediately deleted the app from his phone again.

But he'll acknowledge an evolved approach in several areas. On defense, that includes some schematic additions to his playbook. In conversations with Brown during the offseason, they discussed a game in Orlando from February, when the staff decided, on the fly, to deploy a triangle-and-2 on Terrence Ross and Evan Fournier, which threw the Magic out of whack.

"We had never even practiced it, just drew it up in the huddle," Kerr said. "But that's the thing about it. It's really simple. You just have to have a couple basic rules. We didn't do it again the rest of the year. We hardly do it now. But the overall theme is how you can disrupt teams from their patterns. That's what Mike, I and the staff have learned the last couple years as the league has gotten more and more difficult defensively."

Kerr thought about that Orlando game. He remembered the box-and-1 that Nick Nurse and the Raptors put on Curry in the 2019 NBA Finals. He has seen the league's trend and has modernized his approach.

"I just felt like the NBA game is so rhythmic and pattern-oriented and these players all run the same stuff," Kerr said. "You go from one game to the next and everyone is running high screen-and-roll, high pins, all the same stuff. You see these patterns. So to be able to mix it up is important. There is so much shooting, it's hard to guard everyone man-to-man and still take teams out of their rhythm. Teams are used to seeing blitzes. When they get used to playing against certain things, it gets harder to break a rhythm. So we decided to do more stuff to break rhythm."

He used a zone defense in the opening week of the season. Against Atlanta, they deployed a box-and-1 against Trae Young that worked well. Against Brooklyn, they dialed up a pre-planned triangle-and-2 on Durant and Harden for select possessions.

Here's an example. You can see Kerr call it out from the sideline. Gary Payton II — an underrated key in this defensive start — picks up Harden full court. Andrew Wiggins is hounding Kevin Durant way past the 3-point line. Behind them, Curry is the top of the triangle, while Porter and Green make up the base.

That rare defensive look seems to catch the Nets a bit off guard. Harden wanders out of the action. Durant drags Andrew Wiggins out into an isolation setting, but quickly realizes, as he drives, Curry is waiting right behind for a quick double either direction he goes. Here's the first part of the possession.

That forces Durant to get the ball out of his hands. The possession ends with a half-hearted Blake Griffin post-up and 14-foot fadeaway over a strong Porter contest. In 2021, this is exactly

what you want. Said Kerr: "I learn every night watching League Pass. If you're not paying attention, you're not going to grow with the game. The box-and-1 that Nick (Nurse) ran in the '19 Finals was a good example of forcing you to do something totally different."

Around the team, many of the voices that matter indicate that Brown's influence shouldn't be undersold. According to Draymond, he "holds guys accountable like I haven't seen before in this league on the defensive end."

Again, that word. Accountability. But what exactly makes that tangible in this instance?

The Warriors' analytics staff has put together a defensive metric for each player. It's a muddled formula that takes into account performance in isolation settings, how well you hold your assignment above or below his normal shooting average and some other defensive factors, spitting out a number for every player that can be improved or hurt depending on performance.

Brown makes everybody's number public. The entire team knows who is doing well and who isn't, who is improving and who is slipping. He's direct. He will call you out in film, backed by his boisterous on-court leader.

"Mike Brown challenged everyone," Green said. "He has this little metric sheet guys are on. He's challenging guys every day. Every game there's a defensive play of the game. There's a defensive play of the week. Player of the month. All these things. He's making it fun and competitive. I think that's incredible."

Green has to win all those awards, right? Nope. Not according to him, at least.

"I get no love," Green said. "I don't know who won player of the week, but Otto won player of the month. Play of the game is somebody else every game. But I never get that either. I get no love from Mike Brown."

Porter arrived to the Warriors with a bad habit of letting his guy drive past and then going for the lazy wrap-around steal attempt. You've probably seen it in pick-up games. It's a common fake hustle move. But he's snapped that habit and is more

often sliding with drivers, staying on their hip and funneling them into help.

Those are the type of incremental improvements that, accumulated all together, can lead to the NBA's best statistical defense in a half-decade, despite personnel that doesn't scream 2004 Pistons.

"There are a few things we're doing differently, but what we're really doing is continuing a long tradition of great defense," Kerr said. "That predates me. The Warriors were great defensively under Mark Jackson. This has been a decade-long period of excellence at the defensive end which coincides with the Andrew Bogut trade, Draymond's arrival and Andre's arrival. But as for staff, you need to keep evolving. Mike has helped us evolve. Some of the changes we've made have just been necessary out of a need for new ideas, picking up with what was already built the last decade. ▬▬▬

More Than Desire

Klay Thompson Has a Vulnerable Moment After Warriors Win

By Marcus Thompson II

NOVEMBER 27, 2021

Players and coaches from the Warriors and Blazers had already shared their hugs and disappeared into the tunnel. Avicii's dance remix "Levels," the Warriors' traditional post-victory song, had already finished thumping through Chase Center speakers and given way to the the ambient sounds of dispersing-crowd chatter. Those privileged enough to have postgame passes had already filed into the reserved section for meet-and-greets.

And the entire time, Klay Thompson was affixed to the Warriors' bench. For 35 minutes, he sat.

He began hunched over in his seat, his elbows on his knees, his hands clasped together as he stared at the hardwood in front of him. The fans not yet cleared out of the arena began chanting his name. "Thomp-Son! Thomp-Son!" His head nodded to their cadence. He pumped his fist to a yell of "Klay, we love you!" from the rafters, tapped his heart in response to another adoring shout. Eventually, he returned back to still, gazing at the court. Perhaps visualizing himself on that very floor, which he has yet to christen.

You just know he can feel the ball slide through his hands as he transitions from catching to shooting. See the defender flying at him, obscuring his view of the rim and forcing him to rely on technique and muscle memory. You know he can almost taste the adrenaline rush of anticipation as the ball spins in the air.

But he can't actually experience it. Not yet. It's still just a vision, one crafted from memories and so profound within Thompson, they weighted him down right there on the bench. For 35 minutes, he sat.

"He's right there," Draymond Green said. "He's right there, getting towards the end of the road — or beginning of the road, however you choose to look at it. You know, he has these days from time to time. I understand it as far as I can understand without going through it. I don't know many people that love basketball the way Klay loves basketball. That love competing the way he loves competing. I always talk about our dominoes games. He even loves doing that, and he's severely outmatched. He's just a competitor. One of the biggest competitors I've ever been around in my life."

This was Day 898 since he last played an NBA game. And it was a rough one for Thompson, even though the Warriors beat Portland 118-103 to improve to 17-2. Perhaps especially because they beat the Blazers, a frequent victim in this Warriors era of greatness and a team sentimentally connected to Thompson's childhood days in Portland.

This is more than something he wants. More than hope. More than desire. The postgame image Friday of Thompson was one of desperation. A live illustration of the hard-to-watch side of mental toughness. Not even the $37,980,720 he's making this season can prevent this struggle.

This is what it looks like when the thing that gives one purpose is snatched away. For Thompson, it was then placed close enough to smell but too far to grasp. And he is just genuine enough not to hide in these moments. Vulnerable enough to share this aspect of his trying journey. Though he may not be doing such intentionally, Thompson's willingness to be this transparent allows a fan base to suffer with him. And there is no better preparation for his triumphant return than being able to sit with him in his low moments. Mourn with one who mourns, then rejoice with one who rejoices.

Thompson reclined in the chair, stretching back far enough to point his face to the rafters. He put the towel over his face as he exhaled, his best attempt to let the emotions travel through him. Eventually, he returned to the thinking pose, elbows on his knees as the thoughts scrambled behind his eyes. This time, he put the towel over his head, covering his face. Occasionally he used it to wipe his eyes.

As the night went on, as the workers came to clean the aisles, as Oakland native Damian Lillard emerged to greet his large contingent of guests, Thompson remained glued to the bench, paralyzed by his obvious distress. For 35 minutes, he sat.

This wasn't the first time. Last season, in a home win over Denver, Thompson was a bit overwhelmed too. It was the first time Chase Center had fans since the start of the pandemic. It was enough for Stephen Curry to venture to the back of the Warriors' socially distanced bench and console his backcourt mate. That was day 681.

Thompson is progressing towards getting back on the court. Green said the improvement on the court, compared to when he started playing three-on-three in practice, was night and day.

But it's the closeness that is making this so much more difficult.

"I think going into this particular season," Curry said, "and him getting closer than he's ever been to getting back on the floor, I kind of predicted this would be the hardest part on his journey. Because he's got the basketball back in his hands every day, he's feeling like himself, he's playing pickup, he's around our practices, he's back with us in those type of situations. but he's still not on the court. The good thing is we're talking weeks instead of months now."

After a while, Khalid Robinson, Steve Kerr's special assistant, came out and sat on Thompson's right. Before long, Kerr was on the bench, sitting to Thompson's left. The coach gave his off guard a pat on the back, and some encouraging words, but mostly seemed to listen and just keep Thompson company. Assistant coach Chris DeMarco, who came out with Kerr, stood in front of Thompson, adding the support of another friend. Robinson eventually gave up his seat to Curry, who came from the locker room to sit with Thompson. Green, after stopping in the friends and family section, made his way over to spend time with him, too.

There, they huddled around their wounded superstar.

"After almost three full calendar years off the floor, it's tough," Green said. "So we sympathize with him. But we have to be right there. Continue to push him. Continue to get him to the finish line, or the start line, as I said before. ... It's beautiful to watch him conquer this journey that he's been on. He's conquering it."

It's perhaps a bit sad. Thompson is definitely presenting a unique window into the anguish athletes endure while rehabbing. And having gone through an ACL rehab followed by an Achilles rehab is essentially torture for Thompson, who has said he hasn't dealt with much adversity. But this is part of the coming back. This is what overcoming looks like sometimes.

A successful rehab isn't one absent of such lows, but one that presses on despite them. Thompson, who often presents so unflappable and unfazed, especially in Game 6s, has been stacking up some lows.

Day 525, the day he tore his Achilles, had to be the worst, even more devastating than Day 1. And who knows the private days that were filled with despair and doubt and fear. But he's getting through them.

"Super proud of the way he's just approached this two-year window," Curry said, "because unless he wants to write a book and tell every step of the way, nobody will understand what he's been through away from the game so long. And it shows how much this game matters to him. It's rare these days to have somebody as pure as Klay just feel every bit of what basketball brings to him."

Thompson has been more present through the Achilles rehab than he was during his ACL. He's spent more time in the Bay and with his teammates. His presence looms large despite his lack of playing. And he's become more open this time around, from his boat excursions on Instagram to him talking about his process for staying sane through it all.

The Warriors season opener this year was day 860. Thompson did his best to be patient after shootaround in Los Angeles. He chatted with rookie Moses Moody on the sideline while his teammates got up some final shots. But eventually, Thompson kicked everyone off half of the Staples Center court. It was his time to work.

He even had the music changed. "Put on Tupac. 'To Live and Die in L.A.'," he yelled. His request was granted instantly. Soon, he was drilling jumpers to the beat crafted by Quincy Jones III, and it was clear Thompson was getting his mind ready for the inevitability of playing. "This is such a great song," he said as he walked to his next drill spot on the floor, nodding his head.

He was two months away by most projections. But that shows how this has been an elongated ramp-up. So much has been brewing in Thompson's psyche for months now, as getting back on the court with his guys becomes more and more tangible.

But being close has its drawbacks. The carrot was close enough to tickle his nose on day 898.
He wanted to guard Lillard. He wanted to make the 3-pointer that quelled the Blazers' run in the fourth quarter. He wanted to turn to the crowd and command it to its feet as the Warriors put the game away.

Yet he can't. Still. Thompson was forced to reckon with that reality, whatever triggered it, and chose to deal with it right from the bench, where he sat in street clothes. He worked through the angst. Through the hurt. Through the frustration. Through the powerlessness.

So for 35 minutes, he sat. And because of his willingness to be vulnerable, he wasn't alone. Warriors fans got to be there with him.

At 9:54 p.m., surrounded by his championship cohorts, Thompson finally stood up. He walked off the Warriors bench and disappeared through the tunnel. With a smile on his face.

Day 899 is a new one. Thompson will be ready for it. ▬▬▬

Klay Thompson

'It's Impossible to Know Him and Not Love Him'

By Jayson Jenks, Rustin Dodd and Anthony Slater

AUGUST 23, 2021

The 2020-2021 NBA season missed one thing: Klay Thompson.

So The Athletic called up a dozen of Thompson's teammates, former teammates and coaches and asked for their best stories.

Matt Barnes, guard: We had just won the Western Conference finals. Everyone was enjoying everything, talking and eating and having a drink. And here's Klay with two 9-year-olds at his locker, teaching them how to make paper airplanes and flying them across the locker room.

Jarrett Jack, guard: Only Klay, man. Only Klay.

Steve Kerr, coach: When I got the job, first thing I did was I called every player. Klay wasn't responding to me. So I called Bob (Myers) and said, "Bob, I'm really worried that Klay, maybe he's angry about the coaching change. He won't call me back." Bob just started laughing. He just said, "Welcome to Klay's world."

Marreese Speights, forward: We'd go to a city, and he'd just hop off the bus and go to a CVS or Walgreens with a thousand people outside.

Barnes: That's the randomness of Klay.

Lachlan Penfold, head of physical performance: All he wanted to do was shoot hoops and play with his dog.

Speights: He'd talk about his dog all the time. Or the Bahamas.

Jerry DeGregorio, assistant coach: It's impossible to know him and not love him.

Festus Ezeli, center: Because Klay is very, very … pure.

Barnes: Klay is just Klay. He's like a national treasure.

——————— A ———————

James Michael McAdoo, forward: Shaun Livingston would always say, "Never change, Klay."

Jack: We're in Atlanta, and we wanted to hang out at a nightclub. We're all there, texting Klay, and he's like, "Where are you guys at?" I'm like, "Yo, we're over here." He's like, "Cool, I'm about to meet you guys." So Klay comes, but when he walks in, he walks in by himself. I'm like, "Yo, man, how did you get here?" He's like, "Yeah, man, I was hanging out at this bar, some people asked me where I was going, they said they were going to the same place, so, shit, I just hopped in the cab and split a cab with them." I'm like, "What people?" He's like, "That couple over there." And it was like two married, middle-aged White people.

Speights: We were all in Miami one trip. So we all go to dinner and then everybody goes their separate ways. We all come back to the hotel, and some kind of way, Klay's in the room. He comes out and his whole eye (is bruised). So it's like: "Klay, what happened? We just got back. How did you do that?"

Ezeli: Sometimes he's a little air-headed.

Speights: So we looked at him and were like: "Klay, what happened? Somebody beat you up or something?" He's like, "Nah, I tripped over the dresser and hit my head on it."

Ezeli: Never change was both good and bad.

McAdoo: In the preseason we would go to San Diego. We would always stay at ridiculous hotels. One time, I went out to the beach. Took my towel and went out there and was just taking in the sunset. So I'm just laying down there, and out of nowhere I see Klay down there by the water, just walking, by himself. Just going for a nice healthy walk right along the shore.

Barnes: He's unapologetically him.

Mike Brown, assistant coach: I know the manager of one of those restaurants over there on the water. The Ramp. Klay and I were talking and he was like, "Mike, you know anywhere I could dock my boat?" I'm like, "Yeah, I know the manager of The Ramp."

He asked if I could connect them. I was like, "Sure," but I was still in the process of that.

Benjamin Giler, general manager of The Ramp: Klay was kind of sneaking around. He's this big tall guy, hella athletic. And he was kind of just walking around, and we were like, "Klay?" And he was like, "Well, yeah, it's me." He was like: "Who do I talk to about getting a spot? This would be great for me if I could just go to games from here."

Brown: Literally the next practice, Klay comes up: "Oh, hey, Mike, appreciate it!" I'm like, "For what?" He's like, "Yeah, yeah, I parked my boat there." He parked his boat there without asking.

Jason Thompson, center: I was going to San Jose with Klay, and I wasn't sure if we wanted to drive up there and follow each other. He's like, "Nah, man, let me know where you're at and I'll come get you, and we'll go together." So then he was like, "Yo, I'm here." I'm living in an apartment complex where they have valet, so he pulls up, and I'm like, "Yo, where you at?" At this time, I think he had just signed his second deal. I didn't know what car he drove. He's like, "Yo, bro, I didn't drive, I'm in an Uber." So I'm looking for like a black car and a Prius is just chilling in the front. I'm like, "That's probably one of the neighbors." He sticks his head out and is like, "Yo, bro. You ready?"

Speights: He don't care about no Uber Black or none of that.

Charles Jenkins, guard: Our rookie year, we used to go out quite a bit. Just in the Bay. My brother was there, and my brother is a big party guy. So there was one time, I was just starting the car, and my brother had to run back upstairs to get a change of shirt or something. I just remember him running back out full speed like: "Fuck driving, Klay's gonna take us. Klay's going, too." I was like, "Whatever." I went to the front of the building, and Klay was in a stretch limo.

Nate Robinson, guard: This one time, me, Klay, Brandon Rush, we all had, like, telepathic powers. The club was so loud, and I looked at Klay, and I looked at Brandon Rush, and it was like we could hear each other's thoughts without speaking. It was so hot in the club. I just looked at Klay, and he just looked at me, and we just got up. "Aight." And we just got up and went outside. It was like we all connected at one time, and we all felt it.

Chris DeMarco, assistant coach: We had a road practice, got back to the hotel, and he wanted to take a lap because it was New York City. He wanted to walk around, grab something to eat. We went to lunch and then on the way back, a reporter stopped us as we were walking by and asked us if we wanted to do an interview on scaffolding. I was in the middle of saying "No, we don't live here," and Klay just goes, "Yes."

Kevon Looney, forward: He did the interview like he was just some local citizen.

DeMarco: He just sat there and was giving thoughtful answers on the subject.

David West, forward (from Instagram Live): The night he had 60, Klay had missed shootaround.

McAdoo: Like, he overslept.

West: He probably said, like, five words the whole day before that game. Then just came out, let off, and didn't do no dribbling.

Scott Machado, guard: He scored 60 when he only dribbled the ball 14 times.

DeGregorio: He had the ball in his hands a total of 90 seconds that game. Think about it.

West: That was the craziest — all he did was catch and shoot the ball. He didn't make no moves.

McAdoo: That was one of those moments where Shaun was like, "Never change, Klay."

———————— A ————————

Penfold: He doesn't give a fuck about anything, except basketball and his dog, basically.

Ezeli: Klay and Rocco. Wow.

McAdoo: Rocco was always with him.

Ezeli: When I got drafted and started hanging out

with Klay was when he first got Rocco. He would always want to spend time with the dog. He didn't even really like hanging out with people. I'd be like, "What are you doing?" He'd be like, "Hanging out with Rocco." I thought it was (a person) at first before I met the dog. I was like, "For real?"

McAdoo: He'd be like, "Yeah, I took Rocco down to Ocean Beach and let him run around." I always used to get a kick out of that because I have labradors. Rocco is not a labrador. He's a bulldog. He's not really a beach dog. But he'd still take him.

DeGregorio: Klay's first contract, they were negotiating, and in the middle he had to leave. He was like, "Guys, I have to go home now, I got to go home and feed my dog."

Looney: We were in the playoffs. I think we were about to go to the conference finals. Rocco just walked into the locker room. He went into the shower while everybody was showering, just walking around.

McAdoo: It was nothing for Rocco to show up at the practice facility.

Looney: I'm like, "We just let dogs just come into the locker room, walking around, chilling, wandering into the showers during the playoffs?" I remember (Anderson) Varejão telling me, "Hey, nowhere else in the NBA could this happen. Only Klay."

Jenkins: Random times, he would just follow through. I would be at his house, and we'd be playing video games or fucking around and listening to music, and he would randomly just shoot without a ball.

Speights: There's a reason he has so much success.

Jenkins: One time, we were outside of a nightclub, just waiting for someone to come let us in, and he was doing, like, form shooting.

DeGregorio: His rookie season, there was a game where Klay took too many 3s for Monta Ellis' liking. During the next timeout, I remember Monta Ellis just ripped into this rookie: "You're taking too many shots. Pass the ball. You're just a rook." That

type of deal. I remember watching Klay the whole time, and he never flinched. He never wavered. The very next offensive possession, ball swings, goes to Klay. He takes the first shot and makes a 3. I'm thinking, "This kid is an ice-cold killer."

Ezeli: One game, I think we were up three with about 15 seconds left, and somebody threw the ball to Klay. At this point, you just hold the ball, right? As soon as it touches his hands, Klay shoots it. I can't remember if he made it or not, but I remember his conversation with Draymond afterwards. Draymond was like: "Yo, what were you doing?! Why would you shoot that?" And Klay said, "Dog, they pay me to shoot the ball."

DeGregorio: I remember our interns used to call him Dexter, you know, the serial killer. He was unflappable.

Ezeli: The first 10 games of that season, I remember Klay struggling. Like, he couldn't throw it in the ocean. He was shooting so poorly at the start of that season, one game he shot it so bad, and he was so angry at the end of that game that he left the arena.

Jack: I'm usually one of the last people out of the locker room, and I look, and Klay's clothes are still hanging in the locker.

Jenkins: I was just hearing, "Klay's gone." I was like, "How?" I think he left before Coach got there.

Jack: So the next day, when I come in, I talked to the equipment guy. He's like, "You won't believe this shit. Remember when I asked you where Klay was and asked you about his uniform? So apparently Klay was so mad, or so frustrated, that he left the arena and drove home in his jersey."

Ezeli: Like, his whole jersey and everything.

Jack: So now, mind you, this is early Klay so there's a bunch of guys that live in the same building. I'm like, "Man, when y'all got home, bro, did you see him?" They're like, "Man, Klay was on the elevator, game jersey, game shorts, game shoes."

Joe Boylan, assistant coach: I remember thinking: "That's awesome. I'm glad he cares so much."

Shaun Livingston, guard: We were toward the end of that first (title) season. We've already made the playoffs. We may have already clinched seeding. There is nothing really on the line. I think we were out in Phoenix or somewhere. We end up winning, but Klay missed the game. It might've been the first game all season he missed. He was out due to injury. So we're all huddled up postgame in the locker room, and he stops us and says: "Guys, I just want to apologize for not suiting up tonight. My bad. I take great pride in not missing any games." I remember looking at Steph. I remember looking at Andre. Those were our captains. I'm like, "Is this dude serious?"

Ezeli: He held himself accountable so much. Nobody ever needed to tell Klay what he needed to do.

———————— A ————————

McAdoo: If there was a guy on our team that had previously played for the other team, Klay would always say, "They didn't want you!"

Brown: If we're about to play the Cavaliers ... "They didn't want ya, Mike B!"

McAdoo: Literally every time, everyone would laugh.

Kerr: He does his homework, too. He knows every single guy's connection to every team. One time we were in Denver, and we get done going through the scouting report, and he goes, "They didn't want you, Mike Brown!" Mike was a video coordinator in Denver under Bernie Bickerstaff in the late '90s, mid-90s. Mike was like, "Wait, what? How'd you know that?" I think he goes through the game notes.

Zaza Pachulia, center: We play cards on the plane. I always enjoyed his reaction when he gets busted. I had a pretty cool moment where he had to write a check for me to pay off. ... That's why he's special. Who can imagine Klay Thompson writing a check? He pulled out his checkbook and wrote it right in front of me.

Ezeli: The other day, he got really into the conversation about like the history of trade, like something where he was like, "Oh, yeah in Japan and Germany..."

Barnes: His randomness is what makes him great.

Ezeli: He just started spouting off history. I'm like: "Dude, what?!? Why do you even know this?"

DeGregorio: The beauty of him: He understands what he likes, he understands who he is, and he doesn't waver from it.

Kerr: He really, really cares about people and the team and the world around him.

Ezeli: That's just Klay. Never change. ▬▬▬

The Greatest Shooter Ever

Inside Steph Curry's Record-Breaking 3-Point Night in Madison Square Garden

By Anthony Slater

DECEMBER 15, 2021

The first of Steph Curry's historic Tuesday-night 3s, the one that tied Ray Allen for the all-time NBA record, was of the traditional 2021 point guard gunner variety.

Draymond Green grabbed a defensive rebound and shoveled it to Curry 90 feet from the hoop. Curry used four dribbles to maneuver into the frontcourt while plotting his patient attack. Green set a high screen well past the 3-point line. Curry used a righty cross to duck behind Green, picking off his defender, Alec Burks. Julius Randle sagged too far back. With a crack of space, Curry pulled up from 29 feet.

That's the off-the-dribble bomb Curry helped popularize this past half-decade, paving the path for Damian Lillard, Trae Young, Luka Dončić and so many other current and future marksmen to probe with purpose, target dropping bigs, perfect the stepback and chuck as often and as deep as desired, out to the logo at any point of the shot clock.

"It's a different game (than in Ray Allen's and Reggie Miller's day)," Warriors coach Steve Kerr said. "But Steph made it a different game."

Curry's second 3, the record-breaker, is the one that'll be remembered most, and it came in a more fitting way. No matter how dangerous Curry is in the more traditional scoring sense — ball in his hands, attacking the defense head-on — he became the most feared and difficult-to-contain shooter of all time because of his elite conditioning, mastery of off-ball movement and lightning-quick catch-and-shoot trigger.

Not many point guards give up the ball before they cross half court. Curry does with regularity. On the record-breaking possession, he passed it to the wing and cut to the right block, where dinosaur centers used to rule the land.

This is a common Kerr play call. The Warriors had Jordan Poole and both bigs dot the perimeter while Curry set a block-to-block screen for Andrew Wiggins' defender. Curry probably sets more screens than any other point guard in the league.

But Curry, after the screen, didn't stop moving. This time, he had Burks on him. Burks is a former teammate and not the most attached defender. Curry knew this. So he darted up to the right wing as Kevon Looney vacated and Burks briefly stalled. He needed only a split-second. Wiggins got the ball out to him. Curry got it off in a flash, passing Allen in the process.

"Incredible shot," Kerr said. "Fadeaway, high-arcing 3. The degree of difficulty was there, the crowd was anticipating it, and the aftermath was more emotional than I expected."

This is where the night got both funny and emotional, where some of Curry's parents, shooting idols, teammates and coaches got involved in the celebration. But let's rewind briefly to the night before.

Near the end of Green's postgame news conference in Indianapolis — about an hour before the Warriors' plane had mechanical issues, forcing an overnight grounding and inciting a Twitter storm from Green about the logistical nightmare ahead — he was asked whether he'd prefer to get Curry open with a screen or get the assist to set up the record.

"Pass," Green said without hesitation.

He wanted that assist, and there was reason to believe he'd get it. Green has assisted on 479 of Curry's 3s, more than 300 ahead of the next-closest teammate (Andre Iguodala). But in the moment of truth, when Kerr dialed up that block-to-block screen to get Wiggins a post-up, the scoring forward who had handed out an assist to Curry only 10 times all season found the golden ticket.

"Wiggins never passes on that play!" Green said.

"We run that play a lot," Curry said. "I think that's the first time."

"That play?" Wiggins said. "It's a bucket first. But I saw Steph with a little bit of space and a chance to make history …"

In recent days — in the middle of what Curry called a "long week" of agonizing and obsessing over the record — he rewatched the 2011 clip when Allen passed Miller. There's plenty in it, including a younger Kerr, working as a TNT broadcaster, seated right next to Miller when Allen comes over to hug him.

But after Allen hit the record-breaking 3, play didn't stop. In fact, Kobe Bryant came down the next possession and attacked Allen in the midpost, a very Bryant thing to do.

"He hit it, play kept going on," Curry said. "Eventually, there was a foul. Crowd went nuts. He went over and hugged Reg. They went to a timeout (later), PA announcer announced the record, and he went back over to talk to Reg, his family, his wife and all that. I figured that'd be the vibe (for me)."

But Kerr planned it differently. In the hours before the game, he and his staff decided they'd direct a player to commit an immediate foul after Curry broke the record: then Kerr would call timeout. Looney ended up taking the foul, which seems fitting, since Looney is now in his sixth season as Curry's teammate and does a ton of the unnoticed grunt work.

"You have to do something," Kerr said. "You can't just keep playing. I was hoping we weren't going to be in the bonus. Because I didn't want to give them two free throws. But it felt like the right thing to do. It set everything up for what I noticed was an extra-long timeout. That was organized beforehand, which we didn't know. A 3 1/2-minute timeout."

"I didn't know," Green said. "I thought that was beautiful. Beautiful of the Knicks organization, and beautiful of the NBA to allow that to happen."

Green, arms in the air before the shot even hit the bottom of the net, received the first hug. It was a

long one. After the game, Curry gave Green and Iguodala new Rolex watches as a show of gratitude.

"The only thing missing for me is Klay (Thompson) not being here," Green said. "Just the road traveled to get here. Klay was a huge part of it. If anything could've been different, it would've been that. But other than that, very, very, very special night for a special person."

— A —

Curry was greeted by Iguodala and Kerr, among a bunch of others, on his way to the bench. He teared up for a bit before composing himself, getting the ball from Kerr and delivering it to his father, Dell, seated near the court.

"I knew where he was," Steph said.

He had a moment with his mother, Sonya, and then met up with Allen and Miller at center court. Miller was calling the game for TNT, and Allen had found a brief break in his coaching schedule to fly up and attend the game.

This type of celebration nearly didn't materialize. Three games ago, back in San Francisco, when Curry was 16 3-pointers away, he came out chucking, as the world had ambitiously prognosticated that he could hit 16 and snag the record at home. He didn't. Curry instead went 6-of-17 that night and, frustrated, declined to talk to reporters afterward, a rarity.

He needed 10 when the trip opened in Philadelphia, a manageable feat. The season before, he had hit 10 3s against the Sixers on the road. But Curry, still sputtering, went 3-of-14, and the struggling Warriors offense lost, with some internal belief that the record chase was making the team play worse.

The franchise had initially planned to rest Curry in Indianapolis, ensuring he would break the record in Madison Square Garden. But he'd hit only three 3-pointers against the Sixers, so he was seven away, plus there was a growing sense within the Warriors that they'd been prioritizing individual achievement over team success. So they instead greenlit Curry to play against the Pacers and went for the win.

Curry hit six 3s against Indianapolis and nearly made a seventh in the closing seconds to tie the record. Had it gone to overtime, or had he been hotter, Curry very easily could have claimed the record against the Pacers. They had accepted that outcome, but the alternate reality rewarded the prolonged wait.

Dell Curry, Allen and Miller weren't in Indianapolis. TNT wasn't televising that game. Gainbridge Fieldhouse isn't Madison Square Garden. So much of the celebration couldn't have happened the night before.

"No better scenario than having Ray in the building and Reggie on the call," Curry said. "My family here. It was awesome. … I think everyone talks about the greatest shooter ever, that conversation. My respect for Reggie and Ray, guys who set the bar for what it meant to be a sharpshooter, have the longevity, I've tried to own that in my journey — range, volume, efficiency. I pride myself on shooting a high percentage, I pride myself on that helping us win games. Now I can pride myself on the longevity of getting to that number Ray set, hopefully pushing it to a number nobody can reach. I never wanted to call myself the greatest shooter until I got that record. I'm comfortable saying that now." ▬▬

Gary Payton II

Young Glove and The Glove, a Fit Forged Through Tough Love and Time

By Marcus Thompson II

APRIL 15, 2022

Gary Dwayne Payton II, at one point, wanted no part of The Glove.

He was the opposite of his younger brother in that way. Julian is a reincarnation of their dad and was always enamored by the mystique. But Payton was ready to renounce his rights to the throne. It was too weighty. The comparisons and the pressure. The clawing for every inch. The expectations of a fire-breathing father. He wanted a wall of separation, giving him access to his dad but shielding him from the persona.

Just wearing the same name was too much. Restricting. Suffocating. The glove didn't fit. He wanted his independence.

"He hated his name," said Payton's mother, Monique. "He wanted to be called Dwayne and not Gary."

Now when you see them, they are all smiles. A father beaming with pride about his son. A son glowing from his father's approval. Big Gary and Little Gary. The Glove and Young Glove.

To see them hanging out in Chase Center after Warriors' games, chatting with friends and engaging with fans, it just fits. There's enough warmth between them to melt the moments into cheesiness. After one March game in San Francisco, the Hall of Famer — styling in a white sweatsuit with a purple T-shirt and white and purple Air Force Ones — was the main attraction in the relaxed postgame atmosphere after the Warriors beat Milwaukee. The elder Payton honored every request for a photo, and each time grabbed his son to jump in. The vociferous legend morphed into a meek dad deflecting shine onto his NBA journeyman son.

One of the underrated dilemmas of rags-to-riches tales — specifically pro athletes from meager backgrounds — is the rearing of their children. They want to bequeath the work ethic and toughness at the root of their success. But they also provide a life of comfort, of no wants with few hardships. How do they infuse the same grit, relentlessness and perseverance into offspring they've spared from the very adversities that tend to produce those qualities? Obviously, such intangibles aren't exclusively connected to struggle, as many from affluent backgrounds have been endowed with the same characteristics. But those who tugged their own bootstraps tend to favor the method they know works.

The Glove was groomed by Oakland's energy, by confidence extracted from cracks in the concrete, by parents who were entrenched in the inner city struggle to save their baby boy and others from the clutches of the crack epidemic. How does he make over $100 million in a 17-year career and still put that into his son?

The difficulty of the assignment is why the father beams. Because watching his son play — for his dad's hometown team, no less — makes it clear the mission is accomplished. He has it in him. No question.

It was quite a journey to get here. One of tough love. Of cold nights in a giant's shadow. Of pressure that comes with legacy. The ease they enjoy with each other now was earned, and everything changed for Payton when he embraced what he for so long avoided.

The edge he plays with, the defensive instincts, the aggressiveness, the work ethic, they were in him all along. But before he picked up his father's craft in earnest, before he could embark on the winding road leading him into this season's playoff rotation with Golden State, Payton had to confront The Glove. Not his father, but the enormous persona hovering over his life. And his dad had to let him handle it his own way.

The end result is the son being more like his father than he ever imagined.

"We finally understood each other," Payton said. "I didn't have what he had growing up. He didn't have what I had. It was just, like, you gotta let me be me and figure this shit out. We grew together. We bumped heads back in the day. Just because that's what fathers and sons do, you feel me? We matured."

Whenever a Warriors practice includes some scrimmaging, Payton goes straight to Stephen Curry, one of the great offensive weapons of all time. That's who he wants to defend if he has his druthers.

"It's either him or Klay (Thompson)," Payton said. "But mostly I just go to 30. That's what I want. Just me and him. That's fun."

Defending Curry is what he most looked forward to in the training camp preceding this season. But a hernia procedure shut Payton down and snuffed out his plan. He didn't get his wish until two months later, when a COVID-19 outbreak on the Nuggets prompted the NBA to postpone a Golden State game at Denver. The Warriors, two days before New Year's, instead held a full practice with scrimmaging. It was a belated birthday present for Payton, who turned 29 in December. Chasing Curry around all practice was the gift. No better way, in his mind, to prepare for the elite guards he has to defend.

Payton doesn't say much on the court, but his defense is loud. He mimes his trash talk with his style of play. He's so quick and light on his feet, it's more like creeping. As soon as the player he's guarding gets the ball, or even before, he sneaks upon him like a cat burglar.

Pressuring the ball, especially so far away from the basket, is risky in the NBA. Offensive players are so good, so athletic, that playing them too close could get a defender burned. But Young Glove, it seems, is unconcerned about getting beat. He invites the smoke like a chimney. As if he knows he has the speed to keep up, the strength to stay close. Plus, he wants the man he's guarding to feel him, to be uncomfortable.

"Now he knows the toughness," Big Gary said of his son. "So his game now is way advanced in a deepness over these guys. And they don't get it. Because they are like: 'Man, why are you pressing me up? And why are you doing this to me?' And he's thriving off that. And people fear you. And that's what he was supposed to do."

Payton, all 6-foot-3 and 190 pounds of him, crouches as he gets close enough to see the stitching on his opponent's jersey. He doesn't wave his hands wildly, instead keeping them extended and ready as he patiently shadows his foe's movements, waiting for that split-second window to pounce on the ball. One slip, and he's snatching it.

Oregon State coach Wayne Tinkle said his team referred to 50-50 balls as GPII balls. Because during Payton two seasons with the Beavers, whenever there was a loose ball, he came away with it.

In addition to the ball-hawking skills, Payton also likes being a nuisance. The whole time he's smothering, he's also touching and swiping and bumping. He knows ballhandlers don't like it. That's why he does it, to violate their personal space, to weigh on their focus. All the while looking for a glimmer of frustration — slapping away his hands, whining to the referees, giving up the ball — as markers of cracking veneer.

"He's going to climb into you," Draymond Green said. "The way he climbs into you is almost as if a guy's in your face talking shit. It's probably worse. Because he's not saying a single word."

It's the same mentality as his father, just the declaration is non-verbal. Young Glove is taunting out there, looking to dominate, preying to steal the ball in the most humiliating way possible. Without speaking, sometimes with a smile, he's essentially yelling at ballhandlers to give it up or risk getting victimized by the combination of his 6-foot-8 wingspan and inherited instincts.

———————— A ————————

The one player he didn't get to victimize? His dad. Little Gary has never beaten Big Gary. Pops won't play him anymore.

They haven't played against each other in at least 15 years. And back then, the middle schooler didn't stand a chance. Big Gary did what any dad would do — back his boy down, give him a hard lesson in size disparity and rob his hope with easy bucket after easy bucket.

"He was smart," the Warriors guard said. "He made sure he got (his wins) in early. And then it was just like, 'Nah. I'm cool.'"

And you know The Glove wasn't merely going to exercise his superiority. Even his 13-year-old son would have to hear about it. Big Gary simply doesn't believe in giving passes or lowering the bar.

But, eventually, Pops said, he decided it was best not to play his son.

"He wasn't as good as I thought he was gon' be," Big Gary said. "I'ma tell you the truth. At that age, I didn't want to break his spirits, you know, beating up on him like that. I did it to Jason Kidd. But J. Kidd understood because he was on the streets with us. So what I'm saying is, I didn't want to break his spirit."

He almost did anyway.

Coming up in the game was sometimes tough for Payton. A kid in Seattle while his father was a star for the Sonics, he found it cool to be in Key Arena, around the team and enjoying the ride. He was a ballboy for the Sonics, rebounding for Shawn Kemp and Detlef Schrempf and handing out water bottles. But as soon as he touched the court to play himself, the game he grew up around could be torturous.

He got picked on. Ridiculed. Early on, he didn't play much, which was even more glaring under the spotlight of his All-Star father. Kids teased him about only being on the team because of his dad. He would come home complaining to his mom about his peers mocking him.

"So I told him, 'You can cuss them out,'" Monique said. "Tell them: 'Look, MF, I am not my dad. I am who I am.' This is one time you can cuss everybody out and tell them who you are."

Payton picked up water polo, largely to get a break from the legacy. He was "the only brotha in the water," but it was something his dad had nothing to do with and it was fun. He never fully left basketball, but his heart wasn't fully in it. His mother could see it in his game, the don't-want-to-be-here vibe in his walk. She would implore his junior high coach to take him out of games when he wasn't playing hard.

When The Glove showed up to games, the same energy that made him a magnetic player — the trash-talking, the machismo, the intensity — arrived with him courtside. He'd yell instructions to his son, hurl barbs at opponents, lambaste referees.

"'Dude, you're a parent,'" Monique said, recalling how she'd jump on Big Gary. "'Sit back and just let your boy do his thing.' He would talk to the opposing team, talking about, 'Get him Gary! He's shitty! He's sorry!' It was bad."

The Glove only knew one way, and that was all in. His analysis was straight, no chaser. Where he's from, if you're too soft to even hear the truth, you don't stand a chance to walk in it.

"His dad is a legend, but he's not easy on him," said Todd Phillips, Payton's coach at Salt Lake Community College in Utah. "He came to a lot of our games. I remember we'd invite him to come into our locker room afterward to give some thoughts to the guys, and he was really hard on Gary, but he was also hard on our other guys. He just shot it straight."

Eventually, Payton asked his father to stop coming to games.

The thing about Big Gary was he didn't care if his kids played basketball. He has four children — Raquel, Little Gary and Julian with his ex-wife Monique, and Gary Jr. (five months older than Little Gary) from another relationship — and prodded none of them to hoop. But if they dared venture into his world, he certainly wanted them to uphold the reputation of the family business.

"You don't have to play basketball," said Darrel "Peanut" Jordan Jr., a close friend of the family who formerly trained Big Gary and is now an assistant coach for the G League's Iowa Wolves. "He's always told them: 'You don't have to play basketball. I don't care. But you gon' work.'"

Little Gary, who was diagnosed with dyslexia at 8, wasn't fond of school. He said he kept his grades up long enough to play sports, but they didn't stay up once a season ended. His dad made it clear he needed an athletic scholarship or he'd have to enter the workforce. He wasn't paying tuition only for his son to not take school seriously.

But a scholarship was a tall order considering Payton was on the brink of giving up basketball.

"What I love about his story is that he didn't quit," Monique said. "Because he wanted to. He said, 'I don't want to do this anymore.' And I would tell him: 'OK, so do you want to work? A 9-to-5? Or do you want to work for nine minutes and get paid $5 million? Like, figure it out. Do you want to play? Or you wanna be in a cubicle? Or do you want to play video games all day? Figure it out.'"

Monique and Peanut encouraged Payton to keep going with basketball. But perhaps the greatest motivation came from The Glove.

Pops showed up to a grassroots basketball practice the summer before Payton II's junior year in high school. As Peanut recalls it, that was the first time he heard Big Gary say aloud Little Gary wasn't good.

"He told me I was a sorry-ass basketball player," Payton said. "I was like, 'Alright.' I didn't say nothing to nobody. I just got in the gym with Peanut and went to work."

Peanut had long seen the talent in Payton and, as an undersized player himself, has a soft spot for the type. Peanut would have training sessions with Julian in the family's backyard, and Little Gary would play with them. The biggest issue was Little Gary's commitment to the sport.

The Glove built his career on heart, on getting after it, on pushing his reputation to the center of the proverbial table. Like in the 1996 NBA Finals, with his Sonics down 3-0 to Michael Jordan's Bulls. The 6-foot-4, 180-pound Payton shunned his coach's game plan and gave himself the assignment of defending Jordan, the greatest on the planet. Jordan averaged 31 points on 46 percent shooting the first three games. Being defended primarily by The Glove, the newly minted Defensive Player of the Year that season, Jordan averaged 23.7 points on 36.7 percent shooting. The Bulls lost two straight before winning the series in Game 6.

It's not hard to imagine how Little Gary's disposition might land with his father, thus the blistering comment. Payton knew he couldn't go out like that. Because he couldn't let his father be right. He wouldn't be able to live with knowing his dad saw him as weak, as a quitter.

As much as he despised his father's looming aura, worse was conceding he was unworthy of the name. Making his father proud was still a core desire nestled beneath the frustration and anger. Something about letting the difficulty defeat him would violate a son's inherent quest for his dad's favor.

So Payton decided to spite his father.

In many ways, Peanut was the perfect man for the job. He also was named after his dad, whose rep was big enough in the Oklahoma basketball scene to push Darrel Jr. to baseball. He picked up basketball when they moved to Las Vegas.

When the Paytons moved to Las Vegas full time, Peanut's uncle became the family's doctor. That's how Peanut met The Glove. In 2005, Peanut launched his training business, Elite Basketball Skills, and Big Gary was a client. Peanut was one of the few regulars in the main house at the Payton mansion in Vegas. So he was uniquely positioned to help Little Gary, who opened up about the pressure of his father's prominence.

"I just told him, 'I'm in the same boat.' What I learned is I had to be me," Peanut said. "I told him: 'At the end of the day, be the best you. Whatever that is. Because your dad is going to be who he is. You don't have to be that. He's not asking you to be that. So be you.'"

So Peanut and Little Gary started crafting this unique Payton. Big Gary gave his former trainer the blessing to do whatever was needed. Sometimes that meant showing up at the house at the crack of dawn and yanking the covers off the oversleeping Payton.

They worked on shooting, specifically spot-ups. The Glove was a really good offensive player at the highest level of basketball, averaging at least 19 points in nine of his 17 seasons, and was a career 46.6 percent shooter. But that wouldn't be Payton's game, breaking down defenders off the dribble and getting to the cup. And because he was relatively short, he had to be able to knock down open shots.

They also worked on his slashing and his off-ball movement, taking advantage of his athletic ability. Payton had a habit of just standing in the corner, resigned to being away from the action. Peanut taught him how to use that, to work the baseline and make himself a target. The dunker spot became Payton II's terrain. Sneaking along the baseline was his specialty.

It was the most ideal use of his ability because Payton was the most dynamic of the players in his family. Pops was a scorer. Julian is probably the best shooter. But Little Gary is the most explosive.

"It's something about the Payton kids when it comes to defense," Peanut said. "They refuse to get embarrassed. You could put them on a center and that center is going to have a tough day in the office. Offensively, they're not as gifted as their dad. But defensively, they all have the same mindset."

Part of molding the independent young man included honoring the Monique in him. Payton is following in his father's footsteps but is his mother's son.

She's from Oakland, too. Born and raised. It takes all of 30 seconds to hear The Town in her. Monique James was as tough as she was cute. Her dad told her he knew she was a beast when she slapped a boy in elementary school for taking her brother's sunflower seeds. A self-described tomboy, she was a great athlete who could banter with the best of them.

In high school, she moved to Los Angeles with her family as her brother got into acting. She went to South Pasadena High, where she ran track and played basketball. They moved back to Oakland her senior year because she wanted to graduate in her hometown.

She met Gary Sr. when they attended Skyline High together. He tried to holla, but she wasn't interested. He was too young.

Monique graduated and went to Merritt College, where she kept running track and playing basketball. She set high jump records and, as legend has it, could grab the rim. The bounce Payton has, the eye-popping athleticism, comes from her.

"He doesn't gather and then explode," Phillips said. "He just explodes."

His smile also comes from her. His easy-going vibe. Just like his mom, the intensity is there, it's just embedded in an inviting charm. She was the good-cop parent. She was the soft love to balance the tough stuff from dad.

"He has his mom's demeanor," Peanut said. "Big Gary is going to tell you how he feels. Little Gary

is going to just show you how he feels. Big Gary, if you talk shit to him, he might punch you in the face. Little Gary's gonna take a basketball, cover up his face so can't nobody see it and motherfuck you that way. ... The little Payton, Julian? He's like his dad to an extreme. Julian will give you 30, guard you, talk shit to you and tell you, 'If you want to fight outside the park, I'm ready.' But Little Gary, he just has a different personality."

Ⓐ

In his last two years of high school, while working with Peanut, Payton saw his potential start to blossom. His commitment steeled, and it was producing fruit. He knew he didn't want a regular job. He did have one before, at In-N-Out. He took some friends to a job interview and ended up applying himself out of curiosity. He got the gig and actually enjoyed it. But between school, basketball and regular trips to Oakland to see family, he didn't have time for a part-time gig. He worked enough to be sure about the profession he wanted. The family business was calling.

"He had already got the silver spoon because he didn't grow up the way I did in Oakland, California, on the streets," Payton said. "So when you're being born to a daddy like me, and you got everything — you in big mansions, you getting drove to school every day, you going to private schools in Seattle — it's a lot different. So I had to get in him. That's why I made sure he hung out with me. He was always with me. It was one of the things where it took time because he was a late bloomer."

Payton's grades didn't allow him to go straight to college out of high school. So he went to Westwind Prep Academy in Phoenix. He said the school was "red-flagged," and he still didn't meet the NCAA requirements. So he went to Utah to play for Salt Lake Community College.

He came into his own with the Bruins. Phillips remembered watching him play and feeling like he was a nice player. Skinny but athletic. An interesting prospect. Nothing eye-poppingly special.

"But once he got to campus," said Phillips, the Bruins' former coach, "from Day 1 we realized there's something different about him. ... I remember from the first day we had him here on campus, he just moved differently."

Payton was a role player as a freshman for an SLCC squad that won the regional championship. But by his sophomore season, he was the main guy, leading the Bruins to a back-to-back title. He was named Second Team All-American by the National Junior College Athletic Association.

All those sessions with Peanut came in especially handy as his body developed. The freedom he had at SLCC, the confidence the Bruins put in him to be an offensive leader, had him ready for the next challenge: playing against his father, who was in his 40s and years past his NBA days.

"I asked him," Payton said. "He was like, 'Nah.'

"I respected it. That's when I was like, 'OK, I'm not worried. I'm fine.' If you don't want to play, that's like a respect thing. He didn't wanna play because he knew. Because, *oooooh*, I would run this shit up and talk all types to him. He'd be mad too."

Little Gary's success in Utah landed him some Division I offers. His final two choices were Saint Mary's College and Oregon State.

He initially settled on Saint Mary's. His grandmother lives nearby, and more family resides a short drive away in Oakland. He could get home-cooked meals, hoop at a Division I school and play for a respected coach in Randy Bennett. And Payton was sure he could dominate in the West Coast Conference, building enough of a reputation in the smaller pond to garner the attention of the NBA. It made a lot of sense — until he took his visit to Oregon State. The atmosphere in Corvallis, the big-time football, the campus — it won him over.

It was clear what he wanted to do. But that would mean leaning into his name. It was time to stop running from the comparisons. Time to embrace the legacy. Time to walk in his father's shoes.

"First of all, it's your choice," his mother recalled telling him. "If you go to Oregon State, they're going to treat you like a king. Your father is who he is, and you cannot run from that. But you're going to be your own person. You're an excellent, wonderful human being. And then your skills are

going to take you to the next level. But believe you me, they love your dad. They're gonna just love you because of who you are. You're gonna make an impact. You're just amazing. You're awesome. ...You won't have to worry about one thing when you go to OSU."

Becoming a Beaver was Payton declaring he was ready for his calling. It was him announcing he was worthy, he was ready.

"I was surprised when he came to the legacy," Payton said. "I thought he was gon' run away and come to St. Mary's here. But he said I'm gonna go to Oregon State. And look what happened. I knew he was going to be a dog then. Now you're starting to get it."

The culminating moment came in February 2016, on Senior Night at Oregon State. Payton had a surprise for his parents. He didn't reveal it until his name was called during starting lineups.

He took off his warmup top and revealed his orange jersey. Only he wasn't wearing his usual No. 1. He set it up so his dad's No. 20 could descend from the rafters.

When he broke the huddle before tipoff, he jogged over to the courtside seats where his parents sat, revealing his surprise. He hugged his pops, who grinned as if angels were tugging his cheeks. His mother stood, her left hand over her mouth, blonde bangs swooping over her widened eyes as she failed to fight back tears.

That night, Payton wore the legacy, and it fit like a glove.

Four months later, a gathering for Payton ended in disappointment. A few friends and family convened at Top Golf in Las Vegas to celebrate his college career and wish him well for the 2016 NBA Draft. But despite making First Team All-Pac 12 and being named the conference's Defensive Player of the Year, he wasn't selected with one of the 60 picks.

Little Gary wanted a brief escape from the piercing eyes and hovering chagrin, so he summoned Peanut to join him on the rooftop. They stood at a railing, looking out at the bright lights and tall buildings beneath the black sky of Las Vegas.

"Everybody is sad," Peanut recalled Little Gary's telling him. "But, like, I'm not tripping. We've been here before. Didn't nobody fuck with me in high school. Didn't nobody fuck with me in junior college. Didn't nobody fuck with me in college. So why would I be trippin? I'm used to this. This is what I want."

He wasn't just thinking like his father. He sounded like him. He was talking trash to the circumstance trying to break him, to the invisible wall of doubt in his way, to the journey constantly pressing him. It was a display of the leathered will his father desired for him, the mettle he wanted his children to develop.

It was to this end his father was so hard on him, to create the pressure needed to make a diamond.

"When I was young, I didn't understand what he was trying to say," Payton said. "Because just the way he was saying it, and yelling, and I didn't know how to handle it. But as I got older, I understood it. That's just the way he is, how he expresses his feelings. I understood it and I took it a different way."

This was why Big Gary's children had to work for everything, despite his wealth. They lived well, had a full fridge with a nice house and all the amenities. But they had to pry the luxuries from his stern grip.

Payton's first car was a two-door 1992 GMC Jimmy that required him to put oil in regularly. He parked it on the street because it was unworthy of the driveway. He didn't get a Dodge Charger until his grades improved.

"When Gary went to prep school, he was treated like a regular kid," Peanut said. "You need a TV for your room? Here you go. You need a laptop for your work? Here you go. All the other stuff, figure it out. So Top Ramen noodles and cereal it was."

It was designed to get the dad's fire into the son. He would need it to burn down the obstacles.

Payton's road to the Warriors, and into the playoffs, was nothing shy of a gauntlet. After going undrafted, he signed with the Houston Rockets and was cut a month later. That led to his first G League stint with the Rio Grande Valley (Texas) Vipers,

the Rockets' affiliate. He dropped 51 in a game against the Los Angeles Defenders in December 2016. After the G League season, he signed with Milwaukee in April 2017. Six months later, the Bucks waived him and re-signed him to a two-way contract, and he played a few games with the Wisconsin Herd in the G League. In December 2017, Milwaukee cut him.

In January 2018, he signed another two-way contract with the Lakers, which included time with the South Bay Lakers of the G League. He finished with the Lakers and became a free agent, signing a two-way deal with Portland before the 2018-19 season. But the Blazers waived him before training camp. Payton went back to Rio Grande Valley and eventually earned a 10-day contract with the Wizards in January 2019. Washington cut him but he landed after the first 10-day back with the Wizards in December that year — after another G League stint. Payton signed with Washington for the remainder of the 2019-20 season, played a career-high 26 games and seemed to be finding his foothold in the league. Then the pandemic happened.

When basketball resumed, he played for the Raptors 905 G League squad in 2020-21 until the Warriors picked him up on a 10-day contract in April. After a second 10-day contract, they signed Payton for the rest of the season. He played Summer League for Golden State in 2021 and came into training camp before this season with a chance to compete for a roster spot. But that sports hernia cost him most of camp and the preseason. He played one game and did enough to earn the 15th roster spot on the Warriors.

That's four teams in five years — plus six G League teams — before finding an NBA home. The same fire that got him through earned the respect of the Warriors' future Hall of Famers, who have put their proverbial arm around Payton's neck and anointed him as one of their ilk.

He kept saying the whole time if he got a chance, he would prove he belongs. He did.

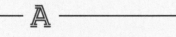

Little Gary is about to play on the biggest stage of his professional life, the NBA postseason, six months after he earned the Warriors' 15th and final roster spot.

And he remained true to himself in the process. His father's tenacity. His mother's joy. His unique style of play. His own story.

"I love it," Big Gary said. "And now your time has come. You worked hard and you grinded. I think this year is going to be that year for him to get that big-time contract and become that player."

One way Payton knows he's made his father proud? He doesn't get those phone calls anymore after he plays.

He used to get one after every game. In those calls, he'd learn everything he did wrong.

"Now I barely hear from you," Payton told his father. "I must be playing well if you're not calling me."

Silence is a sign of satisfaction. Big Gary is old-school in that way. The father doesn't need to call his son when the mission is accomplished. He's an endless well of information, a resource to be tapped. But only if his son wants to tap it. He's no longer yelling from the sidelines, or even offering advice unsolicited. His son is a man now, with his own career. That's all he ever wanted deep down.

The only thing Big Gary is worried about these days is whether Little Gary is coming over.

"He just wants him around," Peanut said.

Oddly enough, though Payton and his father have arrived at this sweet spot of a relationship, the son still does something unique. He refers to his dad by his first name and not by his relationship.

Ask him about his father, Payton will respond by matter-of-factly calling him Gary. When he emerges from the locker room looking for his dad, he's asking "Where's Gary?" instead of "Where is my father?"

Many parents would consider such a sign of disrespect. But for The Glove and Young Glove, it's a sign of their closeness. It's an illustration of a bond centered on mutual respect and friendship. And it's proof Payton doesn't hate the name Gary anymore.

Chris Kamrani contributed to this story.

WESTERN CONFERENCE FIRST ROUND
VS. DENVER NUGGETS

GAME 1: WARRIORS 123, NUGGETS 107

GAME 2: WARRIORS 126, NUGGETS 106

GAME 3: WARRIORS 118, NUGGETS 113

GAME 4: NUGGETS 126, WARRIORS 121

GAME 5: WARRIORS 102, NUGGETS 98

WESTERN CONFERENCE SEMIFINALS
VS. MEMPHIS GRIZZLIES

GAME 1: WARRIORS 117, GRIZZLIES 116

GAME 2: GRIZZLIES 106, WARRIORS 101

GAME 3: WARRIORS 142, GRIZZLIES 112

GAME 4: WARRIORS 101, GRIZZLIES 98

GAME 5: GRIZZLIES 134, WARRIORS 95

GAME 6: WARRIORS 110, GRIZZLIES 96

OFFS

WESTERN CONFERENCE FINALS
VS. DALLAS MAVERICKS

GAME 1: WARRIORS 112, MAVERICKS 87

GAME 2: WARRIORS 126, MAVERICKS 117

GAME 3: WARRIORS 109, MAVERICKS 100

GAME 4: MAVERICKS 119, WARRIORS 109

GAME 5: WARRIORS 120, MAVERICKS 110

NBA FINALS
VS. BOSTON CELTICS

GAME 1: CELTICS 120, WARRIORS 108

GAME 2: WARRIORS 107, CELTICS 88

GAME 3: CELTICS 116, WARRIORS 100

GAME 4: WARRIORS 107, CELTICS 97

GAME 5: WARRIORS 104, CELTICS 94

GAME 6: WARRIORS 103, CELTICS 90

The Stamp of Approval

Newcomers Prove Mettle as Warriors Jump to First Round Series Lead

By Marcus Thompson II

APRIL 22, 2022

When the buzzer sounded, and the commanding 3-0 series lead over the Denver Nuggets was secure, Stephen Curry had one person front of mind: Andrew Wiggins. Having spent the final defensive possession on the bench, he made a beeline from the sidelines, flexing and roaring toward his teammate.

After pointing to the far-left corner of the court, acknowledging the biggest shot of the game, Curry bear-hugged Andrew Wiggins at half court.

"Did you see his smile?" Curry said.

In 2013, on this same court in Game 2, the Golden State Warriors' trio of stars won their first road play-off game. Curry had 30 points and 13 assists, including a drive-and-kick to Klay Thompson for a dagger 3-pointer from the left corner as the Warriors shocked the favored Nuggets. Being in this arena, where it all began, was nostalgic for the Warriors' superstar, and it's the reason he understood the significance of what went down here nine years later. The new Warriors were baptized by fire into the Warriors' tradition.

That's what made this 118-113 win over the host Nuggets so fulfilling. Not just because it extended the Warriors' record streak. They have now won a road game in 24 consecutive playoff series. In every post-season series they've played, Curry, Thompson and Draymond Green have gone into a hostile environment and come out with a win at least once. Andre Iguodala has been part of 22 of them.

But the tradition continued because the new guys around them showed mettle worthy of the legacy. The Warriors have Denver in a stranglehold because more than just the Hall of Famers showed they can handle the moment, the pressure, the adversity.

Wiggins, the veteran who changed his stripes with Golden State, won his first road playoff game by showing some of the gamer mentality required to run with the champions.

In what was mostly a forgettable game for Wiggins, crunch time brought out a side of him that made his future Hall of Fame teammates proud. His 3-pointer from the left corner — the same corner where Thompson put out the lights on their first road win years ago — put the Warriors back ahead, 112-111, with 3:05 left. He had the same shot 33 seconds earlier but missed. This time, after Denver had taken the lead, the Warriors needed it.

Wiggins took his time. He loves the left corner 3, but this one came with the weight of the series on the line. And he drilled it.

"Shot of the game," Warriors coach Steve Kerr said.

Even Gary Payton II was huge off the bench, especially in the first half when Denver was rolling. His defense is why he's on the floor. But the pressure of the stage seemed to enhance his shooting stroke.

Conventional wisdom says role players tend to shine at home while the stars dominate on the road. But in his first road playoff game, Payton made all four of his shots, including three from deep, making the Nuggets pay for leaving him wide open.

"Everybody's not made for the playoffs," Green said. "You look around the league, everybody's just not cut out for the playoffs. You know GP is showing that (he is) with his toughness and with the mindset that he has. ...

"You gotta give credit to guys who show up in the playoffs because this is just not a normal thing around this league. You look around and some guys that you think are guys are not guys in the playoffs."

Jordan Poole is looking like a guy in these playoffs. He is turning out to be a reincarnation of the young Warriors. Same unshakeable confidence. The same resolve not deterred by struggles and mistakes. Same shot-making expertise with a propensity for making the big ones.

He had 27 points on 13 shots in his first road playoff game. He would've had 30 had he not uncharacteristically missed three free throws. He got the Warriors off to a good start, seemed to stall a few Nuggets runs with timely shots and isn't the least bit shy in close games. He now has 86 points in 42 shots in his first three playoff games.

After the game, several members of the Warriors' organization were rolling their eyes at how good Poole is. Everything he's showing says he's built just like his vets.

"Just being out there with those guys, late in the game and in that moment, was extremely special," Poole said. "Because you get to see how locked in and how focused they are offensively and defensively. How everything matters. Just to see guys make big shots and make big plays, have laser focus ... They allow me just to be me and fit right in with those guys. So it was special."

They were once like Poole. Young and quick. The brightest of futures ahead. Games dripping with audacity. Curry didn't have bulging muscles yet. Thompson didn't have facial hair. Green didn't have gray in his beard. They were so young when this run began in April 2013.

They lost an All-Star starter (David Lee) to injury in Game 1 and then lost the game on a heart-breaking layup from Andre Miller, who beat Green with 1.3 seconds left. And, somehow, they came into what was then the Pepsi Center expecting to win. They backed up their irrational confidence by making 14 of 25 from deep and shooting 64.6 percent for the game.

Curry even remembered that time he got into it with a Nuggets fan. But that was Game 5.

"Obviously, a lot has changed since then," Curry said. "But it does bring back good memories of being on the stage for the first time and playing well. The only thing I'm happy about is in the tunnel, they pushed the fans back, so I don't gotta go at no fans out there."

That series in Denver was the initiation of the streak and the mindset of embracing the antagonism of road playoff basketball. They built on that series, and the road win they got in San Antonio the following series, to establish a particular character.

Winning playoff games on the road is arguably the hardest feat in the NBA. It requires a certain mental toughness. It requires talent. It requires a connectedness and shared sacrifice. They learned that first in Denver.

"Just how difficult it can be and how much collectivity it takes," Thompson said of the lessons that first road win taught them. "Guys can have great individual performances. Those may be hyped up with the media. But it's always a team effort, no matter what series it is. And that's just the nature of basketball. No one can do it by themselves."

When the Warriors' turned to their closing lineup, the game was tied at 107 with 4:27 remaining. The Nuggets were clicking and fighting for their postseason lives. The Nuggets fans, many of whom remember how Golden State upset their team in 2013, were breathing down on the hated Warriors.

We know the champions produce in those moments. We know they love it.

Green got the game-sealing defensive stop. Isolated in the post with five fouls, he stripped MVP Nikola Jokić to force a critical turnover. Then he let the Nuggets fans hear about his defensive greatness. He even had some smoke for legendary quarterback Peyton Manning sitting courtside.

"I don't know if it was specifically for me," Manning said with a smile as he walked the halls of the arena. "But he was pointing in my direction."

Green laughed. "That was definitely at him."

Curry drew a charge and put the Nuggets to bed with a driving layup. Thompson played a team-high 37 minutes, 27 seconds and got his one rebound in the clutch. He also executed a perfect box out on Jokić that led to another big defensive rebound. Iguodala pulled out some of his hops — on a thunderous dunk and for the block on the Nuggets' last 3-point attempt.

Curry, Thompson and Green have been doing this for 10 years now. Taking opponents' best punch. Silencing crowds. Making big shots. Getting the stops they have to have. Feeding off the energy, playing the antagonist. Winning at home is expected. But winning on the road takes a different ingredient.

"Competitiveness," Curry said. "A swagger about us. We understand how to win games down the stretch. Obviously, that doesn't always happen. But every series we've found a way to just

withstand runs and hostile environments, and there's a lot of level of trust in how we do it."

But Game 3 of this Western Conference series showed they've got some other players who share the same fabric. They're a win away from dispatching the Nuggets and getting to rest up for the second round, partly because they have some new guys game enough to keep the tradition going.

Wiggins followed up his big 3-pointer by defending Jokić in the post, getting a good contest in the paint as the Denver center missed the turnaround.

On the next trip down, Wiggins hustled his way to a huge offensive rebound. The Warriors were minus-14 on the boards and had one offensive rebound through three quarters. But when victory was in the balance, when it was time to dig deeper, he beat three Nuggets to the ball and got the Warriors another possession. Poole made it count with a driving layup to put the Warriors ahead, 114-111, with 2:15 left.

"Huge," Poole said. "Huge. Huge."

As he departed Ball Arena, Wiggins was still beaming. He doesn't flash it often, so his smile glows when it stretches.

He has found a home with the Warriors and has become an important figure. He became an All-Star with them. And now he has the stamp of approval from the champions. They saw him under the heat lamps of postseason basketball on the road, and they approved.

"It is a pretty big deal," Wiggins said. "Those guys have been through it all, so to have them vouch for you is big. Hopefully, it's just the first road playoff win. Hopefully, there's more to come." ▬▬▬

Good Night, Denver

Stephen Curry Shows the Drive to Put Nuggets to Bed in Round 1

By Marcus Thompson II

APRIL 28, 2022

First, young Canon Curry gets a bath. Then he gets a book read to him, perhaps "Mr. Happy" or "Mr. Messy" from the Mr. Men and Little Miss book series. Then after singing a song — currently the worship song "100 Billion X" by Hillsong United — it's good night.

That's how Steph Curry puts his son to bed.

First, he got Aaron Gordon behind him, keeping the Denver forward on his back like a satchel before dropping in a finger roll past Nikola Jokic with 1:33 left. Then, with the Warriors up 97-94, one basket from ending this first-round series, he weaved around Gordon toward the middle. When a second defender, guard Monte Morris, came to help, he went around him too, getting to the other side of the key and gliding in for a left-handed layup. Then, he took out his mouthpiece, turned to the roaring crowd and rested his head on the pillow of his clasped hands. And it was good night.

That's how Steph Curry put the Nuggets to bed.

"Steph Curry is a special, special player," Klay Thompson said, "and you'll probably never see another player like him again."

The Nuggets' pride, plus the greatness of Jokic, plus the Warriors' anxiousness all conspired to put Golden State up against it in Game 5. The blitz expected from the No. 3 seed in the first closeout game at Chase Center instead devolved into a tense nail-biter. The 3-pointers weren't falling at the usual clip. Sixth-seeded Denver played like a team with nothing to lose — aggressive, physical, pounding the boards, attacking the paint. Harder than nuggets out the microwave. The Warriors found themselves in a dogfight down the stretch, facing a Game 6 in Denver and intense pressure of the suddenly dangerous series.

This was a task for the closer. Curry scored 11 of his 30 points in the fourth quarter to finish off foe No. 1 in these playoffs, 102-98. He secured the Warriors' first series victory since the 2019 Western Conference finals by putting his head down and forcing his way to the rim.

At the end of Game 3 in Denver, with the Warriors up 114-111, Curry tucked away the Nuggets with a driving finger roll with 40.8 seconds remaining. He capped the play with his "good night" gesture, head resting on his hands pillow, as the Warriors took a commanding 3-0 lead. A closer look at the possession seems to show Curry made the same gesture, quickly, before the play began, as if he was telling the Warriors' bench he was about to end it. Then, he put his proverbial head down, and the greatest shooter of all time shifted his determination to forcing his way inside.

When that same urgency surfaced in Game 5, when it was time to end the series and set the Warriors up with a few days off before the next round, Curry again turned to his drive.

Denver made this an especially proper approach. Curry was 19-for-47 from 3 (40.4 percent) in the series. He made three in a row in the second half, getting himself going and reminding the Nuggets why they're so terrified of his shooting. Denver countered by pressing him with Gordon, an athletic 6-foot-8 defender whose leaping ability helps him contest Curry's 3s. But Curry knew as long as Jokic was on the court, and they could pull him out of the lane, there was little resistance past the first line of defense.

"I think I hit those three 3s in the third quarter," Curry said, "The rest of the time, you try to play that balance of not forcing something early in the shot clock and making them defend. Seeing those driving lanes that — if they are going to try and sell out the 3 and you get a big out there in an uncomfortable position — you can get downhill. ... I saw a lot of space."

What's critical for the Warriors' title chances is Curry's ability to generate offense off the dribble and put pressure on the interior of the defense. His foot injury kept him on the shelf for a month, missing the last stretch of the regular season, and threatened his availability for Game 1 and his viability for the series. But whatever lingers from the sprained ligament in his left foot and accompanying bone bruise was no deterrent when it was time to get to the rim.

This is a critical wrinkle of the Warriors' offense, especially as teams commit to taking away his 3-pointer. The Warriors need a place to turn for tough 2-pointers. Their best place for those is Curry, their chief offensive creator. Even the 3-pointers they get, this season has shown, are much better when they are created by attacking the middle and kicking out. And Curry is their best at that.

"He's got the ball on a string," Gary Payton II said, "and you've got to respect his shot from behind half court. If he pump fakes or hesi, or even look up, you've got to respect it. It gets (the defender) up, and he drives the lane and the defense collapses. It opens the floor for everybody."

He's more equipped now than ever to be dogged about his drives. The last time the Warriors were in the playoffs in 2019, the league was just starting to defend him like security guards on a Brinks truck, prompted by Toronto's scheme in the NBA Finals. In the ensuing years, Curry has gotten more prepared to deal with the attention. He's bulked up, adding muscle to his upper body. His playing weight was formerly 191, 192 pounds faithfully. Now, he plays in the 197- to 200-pound range.

What Denver did to Jordan Poole was get up in him and use stronger players to apply pressure. Poole's slithery drives were harder to pull off under pressure, his first step negated with hand-checks and bumps. Poole started retreating from his drive or would even lose control of the ball. That's exactly how teams used to do Curry. They can't anymore.

"He's a lot stronger," said Draymond Green, who remembers the days when defenses could bully Curry. "When he's driving to the hole, what teams used to do is bump him off his path. Can't move him anymore. ... You have to overreact to the shot. If you're not pressed up and overreacting to the shot, then he shoots, and good luck. But once he put his head down and drives it, and he's committed to getting to the hole, he's strong enough to take those bumps and not get pushed off his path."

Still, sometimes, Curry can be the ring leader of the Warriors' 3-point happiness. They often

try to shoot their way out of slumps. The long rebounds and quick possessions have a way of feeding the opponent.

Of course, at any moment, the 3s can start falling and the trajectory of the game will change. That's what happened in the third quarter. Denver had gotten up by 10 points, turning Chase Center into a den of nerves. It was 68-61 when Curry drilled a 3-pointer from the top. The next time down, he hit another one, cutting the deficit to a point and injecting some energy into the venue.

The Warriors were down 83-79 when Curry checked into the game for the first time in the fourth quarter at the 8:48 mark. He had played 29 minutes and would finish at 38 minutes, his highest total of the series. But there would be no more 3s, not from Curry. Payton would hit two big 3s in his career performance. But Curry's remaining impact would be off the dribble, getting into the lane.

His first possession of the fourth saw him attack Jokic in the pick-and-roll. Jokic had just checked in with Curry and had four fouls. No. 30 dribbled around him. Then, with Jokic on his back, Curry stopped short so Jokic could run into him, drawing the fifth foul on the Denver center and forcing him back to the bench 29 seconds after he came in.

Curry took his last 3-pointer at the 5:46 mark. After that, the switch flipped. He was all about attacking inside the arc. He drew an offensive foul on a midrange stepback against Jokic at the 4:40 mark. With the Warriors up 88-86, Curry put Jokic in the pick-and-roll again, losing Gordon on a screen and pulling up in front of Jokic from 19 feet for a rhythm jumper with 3:31 left. Then inside of two minutes left, the Warriors up a bucket, Curry shunned the pick-and-roll. This time, he just took Gordon off the dribble in isolation, scooping it in with Gordon on his back.

So when the Warriors needed one more basket, Curry knew exactly what to do. With Gordon on him out near half court, he feigned a drive and pulled it back, measuring Gordon's reaction. He dribbled the ball at the top as the seconds ticked, lulling the Nuggets to sleep. Payton came with the screen, but Curry rejected it, dribbling into a trap of Gordon and Jokic. He gave the ball up and

got it right back in the right corner. The shot clock was down to five seconds. He had to go.

But he wasn't taking the stepback jumper you'd expect. He wasn't looking for the dagger 3 as he often does in these moments. He ran Gordon off a Green screen. He faked a pull-up jumper that made Morris jump at him, but Curry kept dribbling left. Across the free-throw line. Down the left side of the key. Gordon and Morris chasing him.

Six left-handed dribbles later, he was at the rim. The last line of defense, Jokic, didn't even get off the ground. Caught sleeping, as if Curry had on melatonin cologne. Much like Thompson did earlier, Curry laid off the glass smoothly with his left hand. With 29.9 seconds left, and the Warriors up five, the Nuggets were finished.

Good night. ▬▬

Draymond Green

'My Reputation is My Badge of Honor': On Fueling the Warriors' Edge Against Memphis

By Tim Kawakami

MAY 2, 2022

The Warriors now once again have a Draymond Green-sized chip on their shoulders, which might weigh down other franchises but actually can work for these guys because, you know, they actually have Draymond Green.

They've been through this before, quite famously (though the last time didn't end so successfully). They're well-versed in the us-against-the-world mindset. It's how the Warriors ride in this era, fueled by Draymond's ferocious energy, ferocious stubbornness and his ferocious ability to test boundaries and the league's patience.

To recap the latest imbroglio: Draymond was called for a Flagrant 2 foul and automatic ejection after hitting Memphis big man Brandon Clarke in the face and then tugging at his jersey as Clarke fell in the first half of Game 1 in the Western Conference semifinals. The league reviewed the call and declined to reduce the penalty the following day.

A few hours after the league's non-move, Draymond shook his head firmly when asked if he's concerned that this incident once again has Stephen Curry, Steve Kerr and other major Warriors figures answering the same kinds of what-about-Draymond questions.

"No, Steph and I have been together for 10 years. And Klay," Draymond said at his lively presser. "Coach Kerr, we've been together for eight. Same guy."

Also: The Warriors rallied to win the game and screamed in exhilaration and a little bit of rage afterward. They're up 1-0, have stolen home-court advantage, and that was without Draymond for the entire second half. That's a lot of consolation. But now Draymond has two flagrant-foul points and is just two more points away from a one-game suspension.

Will this make you play more carefully starting with Game 2 here on Tuesday, Draymond?

"I'm never going to change the way I play basketball," Draymond said. "It's gotten me this far. It's gotten me three championships, four All-Stars, Defensive Player of the Year. I'm not going to change now."

He's definitely not changing now. In fact, my guess is that part of the league's reluctance to drop this down to a more logical Flagrant 1 probably stemmed from what Draymond did after the ejection. He danced off the court and egged on the Memphis crowd, then after the game bypassed the media to post a quick podcast of his reaction to the situation hours afterward. No, none of that was likely to get league officials in a good mood as they reviewed the foul.

"Podcasting is my business," Draymond told the press. "I'm not going to not operate my business. They're operating everything. I have a business that I have to operate. They make their decisions based on ... I don't know what they make their decisions based on. That's something we're all trying to figure out."

Speaking of his post-game pod, Draymond concluded by saying he expected a downgrade to a Flagrant 1. Oops.

"I also said (on the podcast that) if you're looking for a dummy or idiot, look no further than Draymond Green — so my expectations are usually off," Green said with a smile the day after. "That's OK. We won the game."

Curry's response to the league upholding the Flagrant 2 was a little more sarcastic: "Shock!"

A pause.

"I don't know what the explanation was, doesn't really matter in terms of how we feel about it," Curry continued. "But the good thing about what we can do and hopefully what Draymond can do is to put it behind him and continue to be himself and play his game and impact the game like he knows how to do. I'm obviously not shocked."

Do you think the Game 1 referees were goaded into calling it a Flagrant 2 by the Memphis crowd, Draymond?

"Of course," Draymond said. "I think we're dealing with human beings. And human beings want to be loved."

The most important thing is that Draymond now has two playoff flagrant-foul points; if he gets to four points, he'll be suspended for a game. That is

exactly what happened in 2016, when he received a Flagrant 1 in the first round, a Flagrant 2 by next-day league review when he kicked out into Steven Adams' groin two rounds later and a final point by next-day league review when he flicked LeBron James' groin in Game 4 of the NBA Finals. He was therefore suspended for Game 5, which began the Cavaliers' comeback to win the title after the Warriors took a 3-1 series lead.

"Yeah, we've been here before," Kerr said. "I'm always amazed at the rule, that a guy who loses in the first round is subject to the exact same flagrant-foul points as a guy who gets to the Finals. One guy plays 25 games, the other guy plays four, and it's the exact same rule. I'm not quite sure how or why that is the case. ...

"Hopefully we'll have a long run in the playoffs and those are the rules and we've gotta deal with them."

The penalty schedule:

• One-game suspension if you get to four flagrant points in the postseason.

• Another one-game suspension at five points.

• An additional two-game suspension for every point after that.

For clarity's sake, I'll note that technical fouls have a separate disciplinary schedule.

If a player gets seven combined technical fouls in the postseason, he gets suspended one game. Then the player receives an additional one-game suspension for nine total techs, then another for 11 techs and so on.

But as noted, Draymond says he won't change his style of play and he can't change his style.

"Absolutely not," Green said, "because if I take the bite out of the way I play, then we go home early and the points don't matter, anyway. Naw, I don't know how to take the bite out. That don't really work for me. Ask Steve Kerr."

That is, I assume, a reference to the many times Kerr and Draymond have clashed amid the competitive fervor, including the time Kerr and

Draymond almost fought at halftime during a 2016 game in Oklahoma City. And to my knowledge, Kerr has never once asked Draymond to back down from his full-out playing style or personality.

Meanwhile, the Draymond ejection wasn't the only Game 1 call that bothered the Warriors. There was the offensive foul whistled on Curry in the fourth quarter, which Kerr quickly challenged but surprisingly was not overturned. And then in the final seconds with the Warriors up by a point, the ball caromed out of bounds seemingly off of the Grizzlies; but none of the three referees saw it, so they called it a jump ball at half-court. The Grizzlies promptly won the tip and then quickly called timeout to set up their final try at a game-winner.

So there was still a lot of Warriors' displeasure a day later. And that carried through to Curry's response when he was asked if this was just another case of dealing with a "there goes Draymond again" issue.

"Even that question's kind of crazy, right?" Curry said. "Just playing basketball, and he was just playing basketball. And you have to deal with what happens in a game and that's what we did last night. We responded. You see that was why there was a lot of emotion, because of how the game went and the particular call. But you don't have to deal with anything, just play basketball and we'll do it together and everybody brings something different, including Draymond, that helps us win games.

"We don't want anybody to have to change their approach based on anything. That'll be the test for him individually moving forward and for us as a team."

As Draymond noted on his podcast and Curry seconded on Monday, this whole situation was undoubtedly inflamed by the referees, the Grizzlies and the crowd's reaction to Draymond's reputation and history almost more than the foul itself. If it's anybody else doing what he did on that play, it's almost impossible to believe an ejection would've occurred. But it was Draymond. Who then gesticulated his way off the floor and recorded a podcast about the situation. None of which will change that reputation, of course.

So no, he doesn't feel like he's getting picked on.

"Nah. I play basketball for a living," Green said. "Have an incredible family, incredible life. I'm not picked on. There's other people that's picked on. I'm not picked on. I told y'all on my podcast, my reputation is a badge of honor. Not everybody can earn that reputation."

He plays and podcasts with an edge. He wouldn't have a very successful podcast if he wasn't this edgy, frankly. The Warriors cherish that most of the time, live with it at others and never want to stop experiencing it. Because when they're cornered in the most hostile playoff situation, as they were in Game 1 against the Grizzlies, they fight back with an edge. And a bite. Even when Draymond has been kicked out, they carry him around. A chip on all of their shoulders. ▬▬

'I Love the Moments. I Love the Pressure'

The Return of 'Game 6 Klay' and the Persistence that Fueled It

By Marcus Thompson II

MAY 14, 2022

Klay Thompson was livid after Game 5's Beatdown on Beale Street, which saw the Warriors blown out by a 39-point margin. But his anger subsided as Game 6 drew closer. It had to. As awful as it was to be humiliated by Memphis, this wasn't a time for fury. Instead, reflection.

Thompson prepared himself for this elimination game by remembering the journey. The 941 days. The taxing his body and mind endured. The audacity required to make it back to postseason basketball. He said he prepared his mind for the showdown with the Grizzlies at Chase Center by watching highlights of past Game 6 performances, just to remember that rarified air he once breathed. A playoff-record 11 3s and 41 points in Oklahoma City in 2016. And 35 points against Houston at Oracle Arena in 2018. And 27 at Houston the next playoffs, including seven 3s. Even his 30 against Toronto in the NBA Finals in Oakland, before the injury that trenched new depths of his resolve.

He then spent some time with Rocco, his beloved bulldog who's been with him through just about everything. They took in the sights of the Bay Area together. Enjoying the scenery, bathing in gratitude. This time, appreciation would fuel "Game 6 Klay."

"I love the moments," Thompson said. "I love the pressure. I love playing basketball at the highest level. Our careers, we are not singers, we are not actors. We can't do this till our elder years. So while we are doing it, you just have to appreciate every single night, because it goes really fast."

With three minutes left in the game, when Kevon Looney grabbed his umpteenth offensive rebound and found him, Thompson was in his calmest essence. He wasn't overeager, as he can get. No pressing. Nothing forced, not even a dribble. The butterflies from before the game had long fluttered away. He was purely him: in rhythm, perfect balance, textbook form, picturesque splash of the net.

His eighth 3-pointer put the Warriors up by 13, all but sealing the demise of the Grizzlies and beginning the celebration of Golden State's return to the Western Conference finals. But most of all, it punctuated the return of the iconic rendition of No. 11.

His 30 points in the Warriors' 110-96 win over Memphis, clinching this best-of-seven series 4-2, was him reaching the pinnacle again. Game 6 Klay is the peak of his powers. It's not just him putting up big numbers in the sixth game of the series. It's about the Warriors being desperate, in need of greatness to bail them out, and Thompson delivering. It's about conjuring magic right when it seems the Warriors have run out.

The tradition continues. Memphis pushed the Warriors to the point where Game 6 Klay was needed. It's been 35 months since he got to be this version of himself again, to feel this level of intensity coursing through his psyche. But he made it back here. He set out to refurbish what he lost with two significant leg injuries. With this season on the line, he claimed it.

The joy of that reality took over after his dagger 3-pointer. He leaped and skipped and pumped his fist as Chase Center reached new levels of frenzy. Thompson held up six fingers to remind everyone that Game 6 Klay was in the building. This wasn't his usual playing to the crowd, but unbridled happiness. The gratification of overcoming mixed in with the euphoria of victory. People closest to him couldn't help but notice his bliss.

"Well, 30 sounds way better than 27," Thompson said. "On top of that, I had a lot of pent-up energy these last couple years, and to be in this situation and to seal the game there, it all came out. I just know how hard it is to get to this part of the season, and it all just came out for me. To see the Warrior fans, it's a moment I tried to revel in for the few seconds I had."

The return to action was emotionally fulfilling. Playing well again was rewarding. Being in the playoffs was its own validation.

But games like this are what Thompson lives for. He grew to become a player who relishes the degree of difficulty. He wants to be in the biggest games against the toughest foes, taking the largest shots. Game 6 Klay is the offspring of his mentality.

That's why this Game 6 was so special. It's proof he is still the player he believes. It's vindication for never wavering, for enduring the bad days and rough performances. For nearly three years, he's been exfoliating doubt from his system, diligently protecting his sanity and absorbing the lessons of adversity. Thompson emerged from this ordeal an altered man with enhanced perspective and a renewed sense of his capacity. He endured more than he ever has and was challenged in ways he never imagined. And it was all in search of the player who showed up Friday.

This was arguably the most he's felt like his old self since June 2019. Despite two major surgeries, being 32 years old, his lateral quickness taking a hit and the rest of the league adopting a style of play he helped popularize, Thompson promised himself he would get back to this level.

He's wanted so badly to be this player again. He put in so much work to be ready when the next Game 6 knocked at his door.

Sometimes it works against him. He's wanted it too badly, too immediately, and his anxiousness has taken the wheel a few times. Such has produced some clunkers — forcing shots, breaking away from the offense, lots of dribbling. Thompson's relentless belief in himself at times didn't leave room for the inevitable struggles after so much time off. Some concern existed about him trying to summon Game 6 Klay.

What would happen to his confidence if he just couldn't anymore? What if chasing the legend coaxed him into a poor performance? The mental toll of this journey already has been mighty. How much more disappointment could he take?

But Game 6 Klay wasn't born of doubt. He exists because of his willingness to risk failure in pursuit of glory. He would have no use for apprehension now. He pulled up to the biggest game of the season, his biggest since June 2019, wearing some jeans and a blazer on a bike with a helmet over his beanie. Shrinking ain't in his nature.

He made his first 3 from deep, making it clear he wasn't going to pass on this chance to resurrect the icon.

"We went on a two-year hiatus in the playoffs in large part due to his absence and what he brings to the table," Draymond Green said. "I know for most people, that's 3-point shooting. For us, that's a competitive edge that no one else on this team has. I know I get a lot of the credit for that side of things

and just bringing the intensity. But like I tell y'all all the time, (he's) one of the toughest guys and most competitive guys I've ever played with — no, probably the toughest and most competitive player I've ever played with — and it showed up tonight."

The Warriors, after a hot start from 3-point range, had grown cold. A wave of nerves rippled through Chase Center as the Warriors missed 12 straight from deep and Memphis was controlling the game. Stephen Curry and Jordan Poole were struggling with their shots. Andrew Wiggins had a rough half. The Warriors needed some life and to snatch some confidence from the Grizzlies.

It was the perfect moment for Thompson, who was 6-for-10 in the first half and made five 3s. He was still feeling it.

Thompson nailed a corner 3 on a drive-and-dish from Green. The next time down, he curled off a Wiggins screen and drilled another 3 over Desmond Bane. The net barely moved. The next time down, he dropped in an 18-foot pull-up with Bane in his face. Eight straight points.

"From the first shot he hit," Curry said, "it's what he's been looking forward to since he got hurt back in the 2019 finals. It's a different joy. It's a different energy. When you see him getting off, especially in front of our home crowd, it's just fun to watch."

They had an extra sauce on them too. Bane said last week he was the second-best shooter in the league behind Curry. Thompson was appalled at such a declaration. Only his trademark honesty allows him to admit Curry is a better shooter, though it violates every fiber of his being. A second-year player dropping him to third?

"Guy said he was a better shooter than me," Thompson scoffed to an acquaintance in the hallway of Chase Center after Game 3.

This is why Game 6 Klay had to return. Because 941 days away from the game is long enough to forget why he's a legend. He was just reaching another level when he was injured, but he didn't get to stay long enough to secure his seat. So he vowed to remind everyone, including himself. While he's still got some room to go in reclaiming his former greatness, the apex of basketball elitism is delivering when the stakes are high.

After a transition layup past Grizzlies point guard Tyus Jones, Thompson had 10 points in two minutes, 42 seconds. The Warriors' offense was awakened from its doldrums. Memphis was forced to switch Dillon Brooks, its best perimeter defender, off Curry and onto Thompson.

Wiggins got going in the fourth quarter, and Curry scored 11 of his 29 points down the stretch to close out the Grizzlies. But it was all possible because of Thompson. Even the Grizzlies, with all their talent and youthful vigor, met the same fate as the great ones he took down years ago.

"He lives up to his reputation," Looney said. "Whenever we need him in big games, he always shows up. After being out for two years and to have a game like this and close a team out that is that good and take us to the Western Conference finals, that's big for him, for our team and for this organization. Klay set the tone for us, and we kind of followed his lead. When things got slow or static, he carried us.

"We did not expect nothing different from Klay. We were all excited to see Game 6 Klay show up, and he did."

When the hardwood became coronation grounds for the Warriors, and the home team got to breathe a sigh of relief, Poole hugged Thompson from behind. The third-year guard who kept Thompson's spot warm until he returned squeezed the Warriors vet while jumping up and down, yelling "Game 6 Klay! Game 6 Klay!" Thompson was beaming.

He received flowers from the Grizzlies. He celebrated with his teammates and embraced the love from the Warriors fans who adore him. Then he lingered on the court a little longer, allowing himself to cherish what his perseverance earned.

It took him a long time to breathe this air again.

"It felt better (than before), honestly," Thompson said. "Especially with the perspective I've gained from the injuries I've had. To now be able to compete at the highest level and be one of the final four teams, it's a feeling that's hard to describe, honestly. It's truly amazing, and it just inspires me to keep going." ▬▬

Back on Board

Kevon Looney Delivers Biggest Performance of Career as Warriors Eliminate Grizzlies

By Anthony Slater

MAY 14, 2022

Prior to Game 5, the quarantined Steve Kerr informed his coaching staff not to chase down a win if it wasn't there. They sensed a strong counterpunch coming from the Grizzlies in Memphis and had a hunch they wouldn't match it. So when the lead ballooned early in the third quarter, Mike Brown pulled some starters, bringing Steph Curry and Draymond Green back to the bench.

That's when and where the early discussions regarding a pivotal Game 6 decision first took place. Who should the Warriors have in their roving fifth starter spot? They couldn't keep going with Jonathan Kuminga, the rookie. It hadn't worked. Otto Porter Jr., if healthy? Nemanja Bjelica for spacing? Jordan Poole and the small-ball unit?

No. Green and Curry wanted Kevon Looney. They raised the idea on the bench in Memphis and solidified it on the plane back and in the hours before Game 6.

"It was Draymond's call," Brown said. "Draymond and Steph's. It's our job to give our players confidence, and they looked us all in the eye and said, 'That's where we are going to get our confidence.'"

The Warriors staff had purposefully separated Green and Looney in this series. They were of the belief that those two non-shooters together would allow Memphis to clog the lane and kill the Warriors' spacing. In Game 5, those fears materialized. Brown tried Green and Looney together, the Grizzlies had Jaren Jackson Jr. and Steven Adams sag off both and the Grizzlies stampeded that lineup in the second quarter.

"I know the worry was the offensive end, and just how they were guarding us," Green said. "But we were getting dominated from the start. When you look at the (previous) eight quarters prior to this game, we got dominated for seven of them. ... So we just knew we needed to come out and establish an inside presence to start the game off and not worry so much about our scoring. We'll figure out how to score the basketball."

The Warriors eliminated the Grizzlies in Chase Center by a score of 110-96. They won the game and clinched the series on the glass and the defensive end. Looney — and the bold choice to plant him back in the starting lineup — is a major reason they aren't flying back to Memphis for a Game 7.

The Warriors had struggled to start each of the past three games, having tried Kuminga as a starter, only to watch that unit get outscored by a cumulative 21 points. In Game 6, they went up 16-8 before subbing Looney out of the game. At the end of the first quarter, they led by four. Looney already had 11 rebounds.

"I didn't know until (Andrew Wiggins) brought it up," Looney said. "He's like: 'You got 11 rebounds already?'"

The Grizzlies were the best offensive rebounding team in the NBA this season and bashed the Warriors in that category in Game 5. It hadn't been a problem earlier in the series, but once Ja Morant went out, Adams reappeared and Memphis leaned into a bruising style, it became a whole lot more difficult (and important) for the Warriors to keep the Grizzlies off the glass.

But with the season on the line, Looney produced one of the best rebounding performances this decade in the NBA. He had 11 in the first quarter and a career-high 22 in the game. Eleven of those came on the offensive end, 11 on the defensive end. He protected his own paint and terrorized the Grizzlies' goal.

"What's more impressive than the 22 boards is I think I ran him 17 straight minutes," Brown said. "I kept looking at him, because after the first five (minutes) he looked like he was dying, and then the next two he looked like he was worse. I don't know if he could get any worse, and every minute after that I was saying: 'Loon, hold on! Loon, hold on!' And he did."

Looney finished at a career-high 35 minutes. He played the final 17 after only serving as a lightly used backup center prior to Friday night.

"Absolutely incredible," Green said. "We always talk about Loon being the ultimate true professional. This series went away from him. Last series, too. Yet he stayed ready."

The Warriors bet on the backbone that guided them through the regular season, believing that Looney gave them the best chance to produce stops in the half court against a Memphis team without Morant and finish those stops off with a rebound. They only scored 110 points. But 110 points is more than enough if you shut off the other team's water. Looney allowed for that.

His 22 rebounds were part of a historic performance on the glass. The Warriors had 70 rebounds. That's the most of any NBA team this season and the first time a team has gobbled up 70 rebounds in a playoff game since 1983.

"When Ja went down, we realized after last game we have to almost adjust as if we are starting an entirely different series," Green said. "Because that was a totally different team we played against the last, what, three games? It's a totally different team. So, I mean, Kevon, he's been one of those guys that has been a mainstay in everything that we do and no matter what — at any point in his career, when his number has been called, he's been ready. We knew we couldn't do it without him, which is why we were lobbying for him to get back into the starting lineup, and he came through." ▬

'It's a Partnership'

How Steve Kerr, Coaches and Veteran Players Run the Warriors Together

By Tim Kawakami

MAY 23, 2022

Twenty minutes after their team video session ended and players and staffers filed back to their hotel rooms, Steve Kerr stood outside the doorway and gestured over his shoulder to the TV screens and empty seats and tables. There was a clear meaning: This is where some of the magic happens.

That's the symbolic heart of the Warriors' distinctive blend of coaching lifers, thoughtful veteran legends, middle-career players and young up-and-comers. This is how Kerr coaches these players, coaches through the veterans and actually coaches alongside Stephen Curry, Draymond Green and Andre Iguodala.

"Sometimes they have their own message," Kerr said of Curry, Draymond and Iguodala. "Sometimes they'll have a players-only meeting. Maybe after a game or before practice, Draymond and Andre or one of the guys will just say, 'Hey, we need a few minutes.' Great.

"More often than not, we'll have a film session, just like we just did, and the leaders will point something out to the young guys and challenge them, and we'll kind of just hash it out."

The practical results of this coach-players symbiosis have been obvious throughout this playoff run, which, after a 109-100 Game 3 victory over the Mavericks, has the Warriors up 3-0 in the Western Conference finals. And they need this connection. They cherish it. The Warriors don't have the overwhelming talent they had in 2017 or 2018, the foundational guys aren't so young anymore and they have a mix-and-match roster with many mostly equivalent parts that need to be deployed in exactly the right way at exactly the right time.

What's at an all-time level over all other Warriors iterations is the trust and faith between Kerr's staff and Curry, Klay and Draymond as they figure their way through these series. What's undeniable is the accumulated sense of shared responsibility for all strategic decisions between a group of men who have been together since Kerr arrived in May 2014.

"We're at the point now that Steph's 13 (seasons) in, I'm 10 in," Draymond said. "We've all been together eight years (with Kerr). We trust what the coaches say, they trust what we see. It's a partnership. They do obviously 99.8 percent of the game plan. Then, if we have input, they take our input. We like to put our brains together, give them thoughts on what we're feeling on the court, which sometimes can be a little different than what they're seeing. And then try to make it all work together."

For instance: Going into this series, Kerr figured that rookie Moses Moody, who hadn't played a meaningful minute in the previous two series, could be a nice fit for some more minutes against Dallas. So he told Moody. And then ...

"I talked to Draymond after that, and he's like, 'Yeah, I totally agree,'" Kerr recalled. "So I think we're on the same page most of the time, anyway, because we've been together for so long, and we know what works and what's necessary. It wasn't like we had this moment where Draymond and I put our heads together and said, 'What do we do?' It was more like we both recognized beforehand, before we talked to one another, that Moses made sense for this series."

Moody, of course, took Damion Lee's spot with the second unit in the fourth quarter of Game 2, played 10 strong minutes in the Warriors' comeback victory, then followed that up with another solid couple of stints in Game 3.

"Even in that game (on Friday), before Coach had told me I was going in, Dray pulled me to the side and said I'd probably get in," Moody said on Sunday. "Told me a couple things to focus on. It's time to lock in. I listened to that. And that wasn't even the words he said, it was a lot more motivational and inspirational.

"It means a lot. 'Cause I'm sure if they brought it up to put me in and Draymond said no, then it wouldn't happen. Knowing that he's got confidence to put me in ... he had faith in me to perform in there after not playing all game, getting in there the fourth quarter of a playoff game ... that means a lot. ... If he says I can do it, might as well believe it."

Moody probably was semi-joking that Draymond could've vetoed his playing time. He probably was

also more than a bit right on the nose. There's no doubt that the two strongest personalities on the team — in strategy sessions and almost all other moments — are Kerr and Draymond. And both men know it's important for them to agree on important issues.

"It's always a give and take," Draymond said of his discussions with Kerr. "And very seldom do I go against him. I'm like, alright, if that's what we're doing, then that's what we're doing. Because we trust in the work that's been put in. I watch film. I've been watching all of these games and giving my opinion. But I ultimately know they've watched 10 times the amount of film I've watched. We've been through enough battles to where I know, we all know we can trust their game plans. They're going to put us in the best positions to be successful."

Curry has the most important voice in the organization because he's the greatest player in franchise history and also its greatest leader. Kerr is the chief strategist and motivator. Draymond is the defensive genius and firebrand in the middle of everything. And usually, it's Kerr and Draymond having the longest (occasionally lively) conversations. Because they're so similar.

"We see the game the same way, for sure," Kerr said. "I've always had a defensive mindset, which is ironic because I wasn't much of a defender. But I want to start out every game making a defensive stand. And that's who Draymond is; he's the ultimate defender."

The decision to bring Kevon Looney back into the starting lineup for the crucial Game 6 against Memphis in the Conference semifinals was a much more emphatic example of the team leaders speaking up, Curry said. In that case, Kerr was away from the team in COVID protocols and watching the embarrassing 39-point Game 5 loss in Memphis on TV.

That night, Kerr and acting coach Mike Brown talked about possible lineup options for Game 6, and Brown told Kerr that Curry and Draymond already had been pushing for Looney to start as a way to counteract Memphis' mid-series turn to Steven Adams at center. A follow-up conversation between the three on the plane solidified it.

"The Loon call was a little more aggressive in terms of what we feel on the court and the adjustments that Memphis had made in that series," Curry said Monday. "We felt like it was a necessity to give it a try. Loon took advantage of that.

"But any conversation, in our history and experience, there's definitely give and take in terms of what we see, what we feel as players, what coaches are responsible for in terms of what the numbers say and their perspective. Good teams hopefully have chemistry and trust that when you get to a point where you make those decisions, you kind of roll with it and live with the results."

Or here's how Brown put it after Looney pulled down 22 rebounds in the Game 6 series-clincher: "It was debated a little bit, but the reality was it was Draymond's call, Draymond and Steph's. It's our job to give our players confidence, and they looked us all in the eye and said that's where we are going to get our confidence. And they have done it before, Draymond has carried this organization for years with his hard hat.

"Obviously Steph and Klay with their shooting, but what Draymond does, it's unbelievable, and Steve is going to roll with Draymond no matter what he says and what the outcome is."

Put bluntly, Kerr needed to know if Curry and Draymond trusted Moody in a playoff environment. He checked.

"The coaching staff has to know that the guys on the court trust whoever you're going to put out there," Draymond said. "If guys on the court don't trust who you put out there, then it doesn't work. We know Moses works. When a guy puts the amount of work in that Moses does and carries himself that way and then every time he's ready for his number to be called, you have to trust in that and give him his opportunity. Coach trusted him and gave him his opportunity. He took advantage of it."

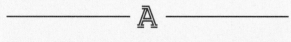

Not all coaches are eager to run strategic decisions through their stars. Not all stars would have the desire or mental energy to sign off on all those details.

But Kerr, who won championships playing with Michael Jordan in Chicago and Tim Duncan in San Antonio, isn't just any coach. And Curry and Draymond are more than normal stars. They've won three championships together and been to five previous finals together. They've won more than any Warriors group ever has. They're still winning now.

"I just think there's a level of trust now with everything we've been through, good and bad, that it's truly a collaboration," Kerr said. "Any big decision that I have to make, I pretty much always talk to Draymond and Steph. Throw Andre in there as well.

"Those guys have seen it all, they've done it all. We've been together so many years. It only makes sense to run stuff by them. And we'll talk stuff out. Ultimately, if we can come to a decision collectively it's great because then we all take ownership of it and we'll continue to collaborate and tweak as we go on."

At one point on Sunday, when there was a timeout after Reggie Bullock crashed to the floor and needed a few minutes to get back up, Iguodala was the one who urgently called the players on the court to him for a brief strategy session. Kerr joined in, but he was happy just to listen to Iguodala, Curry, Draymond and the others talk it over before the game resumed.

It looked like something Jordan did alongside Phil Jackson during the Bulls dynasty. Or something the Spurs would've done during Duncan's run under Gregg Popovich.

"I witnessed that as a teammate of those guys," Kerr said. "It's always a collaboration in the NBA between coaches and star players. It's a players' league. This is not college basketball where you're the czar and whatever you say goes. NBA coaching is all about collaborating with your stars. And that's why having the right stars is everything.

"If you have guys like Michael or Tim Duncan or Ginobili or Steph or Draymond, it's not just about the production on the court, it's about the extreme intelligence and awareness. Ultimately, the collaboration happens because of it."

These players have also lost more brutally than any Warriors group ever has. And they're bound together more tightly now, eight seasons into this, than ever. They haven't drifted apart. They haven't gotten tired of each other. They talk through whatever it is in front of them, and if that works they go on to the next thing. There really isn't another team like it right now, which is what I suggested to Curry on Monday.

"I don't know," Curry deadpanned. "I've only been on one team."

But what a team. It's Curry's team. And Draymond's team. And Iguodala's team. And Kerr's team. And everybody else's team. If you want to beat them, you have to beat them all, on the court and in the meeting rooms. Good luck with that. ▬▬

Andrew Wiggins

With a Signature Performance in Dallas, Wiggins is Anointed as Part of the Warriors' Core

By Marcus Thompson II

MAY 23, 2022

All that was left for Andrew Wiggins was a big performance like this. A coronation of his induction into the franchise's core. It can only happen in the NBA playoffs, where Warriors are fashioned. It was a crescendo of his adoption into the fold. Fittingly, it came on the road, where the Warriors have now won at least once in 26 straight postseason series. Road playoff greatness is the finest quality.

Wiggins had been stacking moments throughout this postseason, thriving in the dirty work and spearheading the defense. But in Game 3, he popped through with 27 points and 11 rebounds as the Warriors took a 3-0 lead in the Western Conference finals with a 109-100 win. His new signature game — punctuated by a new signature play.

What works about Wiggins, why he meshes so well with this championship core, was evident in the dunk of his life. He saw the rim, he saw Mavericks' star Luka Dončić in the lane, and somehow his mind switched to hyper-attack mode. He exploded faster, jumped higher, flushed harder. He wasn't just going for a dunk. Wiggins was trying to snatch a soul.

It's the same go-get-it mindset on which the Warriors have built this era. The same merciless intent to dominate that peaked in the Kevin Durant years. Wiggins is one of them now because they know he's got this spirit in him.

"Fourth quarter, in a big win," Stephen Curry said. "And not just because it was Luka, but because of the way it looked. It was unbelievable."

It was so vicious that referee Marc Davis called Wiggins for an offensive foul after Dončić crumbled to the floor like he was assaulted. The Warriors challenged the ruling on behalf of basketball, because the sport could not stand for such an epic dunk being negated by thespianism.

"That was impressive," Dončić said. "I'm not going to lie. I saw the video again, I was like, 'Ooooh.' That was pretty incredible. I wish I had those bunnies."

Added Curry: "And we got to see 800 replays because of the challenge. So appreciate it, Marc. That was nice."

Everyone who's official has one of these types of games. Andre Iguodala in the 2015 NBA Finals. Klay Thompson in the 2016 Western Conference finals. Draymond Green in the 2019 West finals. Kevon Looney in the 2022 West semis. The path to Warriors lore is through such timely, memorable contributions. Wiggins is official.

The way he has risen to the Dončić challenge on both ends, on top of his willingness to play his role within the core, is illustrative of why the key figures consider him essential. He has proven he will do what it takes to win. Rebounding. Defending Denver's big men. Chasing a flash of lightning in Ja Morant. Picking up Dončić full court. Wiggins is about it.

But winning this series against Dallas, which the Warriors are now a game from doing, required him also going after Dončić. The career scorer needed to dust off his offensive repertoire and use it against the Mavericks star.

"I think the way this series has mapped out, there's space for him to attack," Warriors coach Steve Kerr said. "You know, the way they are guarding Steph and Klay (Thompson), the lineups that are out there for both seems there's some room for Wiggs to attack."

From the opening tip of the Western Conference finals, Wiggins has done so with a swagger worthy of his ringed teammates. The Warriors love going for the kill. From dagger 3s to big road wins, they've always gotten joy out of demoralizing opponents. On Sunday, it was Wiggins' turn to rip the beating heart out of the opponents' chest. He was the demoralizer.

The Warriors' first year-and-a-half with Wiggins, and even parts of this season, was about pushing him to the peak of his aggressiveness while still staying within the confines of his role. He's delivered all postseason, mostly on defense and on the boards. But here, it manifested in his best offensive performance of the postseason. He took 20 shots in a game for the first time since Dec. 28, 2021. His dunk over Dončić served as a microcosm of this series.

"You don't win in the playoffs without guys like Wiggs," Kerr said. "We're basically mirroring Dončić's minutes so that Wiggs can stay on him.

And he's another guy, like Steph, who just never seems to get tired. He's in amazing shape. Wiggs, it's been a brilliant year for him, and it's continued in the postseason."

It's not that the Warriors knew Wiggins would be this. But even in the face of criticism for its beliefs, the front office believed this was possible. If everything fell into place. If he accepted the need to change his stripes as a player. If he could handle the wattage of the spotlight the Warriors are under. Then, he would be the perfect addition.

Not many believed them. NBA stripes tend not to change after six years. But Tom Thibodeau told them they'd love Wiggins. Jimmy Butler, a renowned competitor, told them Wiggins was a rider. And when he arrived in the Bay Area, Wiggins showed some of the elements obscured by his reputation as a losing scorer. His teammates and coaches were won over.

"We knew from Day 1," Draymond Green said, "He competes. It was obvious from the jump that he was somebody who gets after it."

He's been so vital in these playoffs, his contract is now worth it. Before, evaluating Wiggins required not adding the $31.6 million salary for this season to the equation. But his value to the Warriors has been such that even the $33.6 million he's due to make next year seems worth it. The Warriors could very well sign him to an extension this offseason, locking in one of their most integral players. And that wouldn't hinder talks with guard Jordan Poole, also in line for an extension, because any new contract Poole signs wouldn't kick in until after the final season of Wiggins' current contract.

The Warriors are in a position to win their fourth championship of this era. If they manage the feat, Wiggins will have been a critical part of that. So will Poole. And the Warriors would automatically be among the favorites to reach the championship series again next year no matter how this one ends. Nothing about how the Warriors have done business suggests they would sacrifice winning to cut costs. So it only makes sense they'd run it back with those core players next year.

The question is, can they find a salary numbers for Wiggins and Poole that could keep both of them? Wiggins would have to take a smaller average salary and more years. The Warriors are on the books for $37.5 million between Wiggins and Poole for the 2022-23 season. Would they pay $10 million more, before luxury tax, to keep them both? That's not something they have to worry about until after next season. They've found a keeper in Wiggins, and he's entering his prime. There are no plans to move on from him anytime soon.

Wiggins has earned all of this consideration. He's worked for it. He's climbed all the steps. He's been everything he's needed to be. That includes not being the player he used to be. Wiggins has been very clear he still likes to score. But he's been willing to do it in different ways, to wait in line to eat and let the OGs fix their plates first.

The former No. 1 pick still isn't the frontline player he was drafted to be. He is thriving because he is playing with all-time greats. But he has the talent to star in his role and occasionally shine even brighter. He's learning from teammates the value of operating in their collective.

"Some people never get the opportunity," Wiggins said. "So you can't take it for granted."

Not everyone can meet the standard they set. The Warriors have tried many complementary pieces for their championship core. Not all of them, despite their talent, have risen to the level the stars command. Wiggins has done that. He's not Durant, but he's an upgrade over the younger Harrison Barnes, who once filled this same role. And Wiggins is only 27 and just learning about this level.

"Wiggs has it in him," one team executive said. "It's all about the situation and the opportunity. That's the power of No. 30."

Curry is, indeed, the singular force that makes the Warriors go. He controlled Game 3, raining 3s to remind the Mavericks why they're terrified of his shooting. That, in turn, opened up his drives to break down the Dallas defense.

By the fourth quarter, Dallas was back to double-teams of Curry near half court. The key to the Warriors' success is having guys who capitalize. Wiggins was the demoralizer.

"It's amazing to see it happening under the bright lights," Curry said. "You don't know how guys are gonna respond when they're asked to do what we're asking them to do at this stage in the season, in the playoffs, when you have the highest hopes. But he's stepping up and that's only because of his approach and his attitude and just being a gamer."

Before the ceremonial anointing of Wiggins in Game 3, before he could enjoy the spoils of his first postseason run, he became a Warrior through shared suffering.

The core of the Warriors was raised together. Players rose through the ranks together on the road to becoming champions. Which means they lost together. They endured heartbreaks together. They responded together. From getting outclassed by San Antonio in 2013, to coming up short in seven games against the Clippers in 2014, to getting down 3-1 to Oklahoma City in 2016. The chemistry that made them great was birthed through struggle.

After the worst season in recent vintage – 15-50 in 2019-20 – the Warriors set their sights on the playoffs. They closed the 2020-21 regular season by going 15-5 over the last 20 games. It was good enough to reach the inaugural Play-In Tournament. The Warriors then lost to the Lakers in a nail-biter before getting ousted by Memphis.

It was a year ago, but still part of what's happening now. Before Wiggins could win like them, he had to go through the struggle with them. He got to feel the intensity and pressure. Teammates remember how well he defended LeBron James, how hard he played down the stretch of the close loss against the Grizzlies. His offense wasn't spectacular, but his willingness to compete registered. They got to see him in that environment. They got to see him respond. This is how intimacy is developed.

Now, despite this being his first real run, he's got the anointing of the Warriors' champions. They've come to appreciate it when he smiles. They're awed by his athleticism and applaud his humility. They communicate with him. They speak up for him, praise him to his face and hype up his contributions. Their journey together, with him in the mix, is what made Game 3 such a monumental night for Wiggins.

Without a doubt, he's one of them. ▬▬

A Trio for the Ages

Curry, Green and Thompson are Finals-Bound Once More

By Marcus Thompson II

MAY 27, 2022

Andre Iguodala, with his Western Conference champions T-shirt over his light burgundy long-sleeve polo, has a theory about why the Warriors' championship core is underappreciated. They are too tangible. Not just them, all NBA players. He is convinced this all-access era works against Golden State's prominent trio.

Iguodala understands Stephen Curry, Draymond Green and Klay Thompson to be rare gems and even more exquisite in how they coalesce. Yet he watches how people relate to them. He hears how they are talked about. He witnesses them be commodified in the modern machine. And Iguodala can't help but roll his eyes at what people are missing.

Brilliance isn't always meant to be touched. It's properly experienced from ample distance. That's how one fully appreciates the complexity and layers of grandeur.

The beauty of the NBA is how close the players feel to fans, how intimate of a relationship players have with their followers. But it's hard to behold something so frequently held. The luster gets lost beneath fingerprints. Iguodala can see how the overexposure of the contemporary landscape deprives the Warriors' foundational pieces of proper awe. Especially Curry.

"I met Michael Jordan when I was 18 years old at his first-ever Jordan Brand Classic," Iguodala said. "I was almost in tears. Because I saw him. People are so close to it now, and we can just touch them. We can capture them with a camera phone. So it kind of takes away that reverence, and it's taken for granted. They think this can just keep being reproduced. ... And there are so many hot takes and people who have no business speaking on it. It just kind of makes you a little sick. This is the world we live in. But this is something special. I'll say this — in 10, 15 years, people are going to be like, 'Damn, we didn't appreciate it.'"

Now is the time to stop and take a step back. Digest the grandeur in its totality. Appreciate the resilience of this greatness.

On June 13, 2019, Curry, Green and Thompson each walked off the Oracle Arena floor into an uncertain future. Curry was bombarded with defensive schemes aimed at his eradication. Green's offense had declined, and he was facing bigger and more athletic versions of himself. Thompson had a torn ACL. Kevin Durant was hurt and expected to leave in free agency. Iguodala's departure was imminent. Even their hallowed arena in Oakland was turning off its lights. The price of their five-year run was reaching astronomical levels. Some, including many Warriors fans, prognosticated their demise.

Yet with a five-game victory over the Dallas Mavericks, the Warriors clinched a spot in the NBA Finals for the sixth time in eight years. In doing so, they validated themselves, proven by the test of time and the adversity of injury. After two years of missing the playoffs, Curry, Green and Thompson have carried the Warriors back to where they belong and where they promised themselves they would return. Their ability to resume their dominance of the West is proof it was, indeed, them all along: the Warriors Trinity, the foundation on which this whole era was built.

They are here again because individually they are built for the bright lights. They are here again because as a unit, they complement and elevate each other. They are here again because their style of play and the tone they set makes them compatible with a multitude of skills and players, provided they come with a winning mindset.

Back in 2020, when the Warriors were putting together their version of the bubble, their stars opted out. Curry didn't show up once. Neither did Green. Thompson, back from a torn ACL, was done after one visit. More practice wasn't the solution. They knew they didn't need a special camp, secluded from the coronavirus, to reclaim their former glory.

"We kept telling ourselves," Green said, "that when we get back healthy and we get back whole, we're going to do it again. We never stop believing that. We know what we're capable of."

The trio of basketball brothers, bonded by their covenant to win, made sure each remembered their collective truth. While many in the basketball world poured out a little liquor on the headstone of their reign, often using their hiatus from the main stage to impeach their legitimacy, the Warriors' trio kept sharing the same message within their circle. Over text messages. On FaceTime calls. At dinners. In side conversations in practice. In quick, intimate huddles during games. So much around them was changing. But as long as they were together, as long as they had each other, as long as they did what they do, they would win big.

What was true then is still true now: Curry, Green and Thompson — when all three are healthy — have been nearly impossible to beat with Steve Kerr as their coach.

"This one is very sweet just because of where we were in 2019," Curry said. "We never lost faith, but you understand how hard of a process it was going to be to climb that mountain again. ... I think internally we are all extremely proud of what it took to get back here.

"Yeah, it's definitely sweet based on what we went through."

———————— A ————————

By the end of the Western Conference finals, Luka Dončić was running like a man who'd flown across two time zones in a middle seat. His valiant effort to pull off a miracle for his Mavericks, who made Game 5 competitive after being down 25, must've felt like the weight of Texas on his shoulders. Try as he might, the Warriors always had an answer in their 120-110 win, capping the gentleman's sweep of Dallas.

Curry didn't play particularly well after rolling his ankle just over three minutes into the game. But it became more evidence why a team featuring these three is so hard to beat. Thompson had 32 points and became the first player to make eight 3-pointers in two closeout games in the same postseason. Green, the defensive anchor, put up 17 points on seven shots to go with nine assists.

That's the thing about the three of them — taking out one opens the window for the other two. They've endured and experienced just about everything while together. Injuries. Heartbreaking losses. Drama. Each other's flaws. They've grown up together, started families and businesses, in a

sense gone their separate ways off the court. None of it has loosened the fabric weaving them together. Because the common thread undergirding their respect for and belief in each other is their relentlessness. They can bank on the fight in one another. That's why Kerr, just as fiery, can lead them. Their story can't be told without Kerr, the ideal conductor.

"All the pieces fit," Curry said. "Our personalities fit. So much trust in each other. But we are all just so competitive at the end of the day. That's carried us."

Dončić shouldn't feel bad. He is now part of an elite group of players who've succumbed to the inevitability of these Warriors. LeBron James. Durant and Russell Westbrook. James Harden. Damian Lillard. Anthony Davis. Chris Paul. Kyrie Irving. Nikola Jokić. Dwight Howard. Some bonafide Hall of Famers have run into the Warriors and walked away just like Dončić did. Overwhelmed. Having to re-think their plans. Lacquering a salve of what-ifs on their wounded pride.

The Warriors are just the fourth NBA franchise to have reached the finals six times in eight years. They join the Lakers (the Jerry West and Magic Johnson eras), Celtics (Bill Russell era) and Bulls (Michael Jordan era). Of the five major pro team sports, the Warriors are just the 13th franchise to reach the championship round in six of eight seasons. In addition to the four NBA teams that have done it: the Yankees of MLB; the Oilers, Maple Leafs, Red Wings and Canadiens of the NHL; the Browns, Packers and New York Giants of the NFL; and the Lynx of the WNBA.

The Warriors are 22-4 in the 26 series since this playoff era began in April 2013. They've won three series over higher seeds. They've lost just once when they've had home-court advantage.

Here is another way to look at it: Only three teams in the past 10 seasons can make the claim of beating a Warriors team with a healthy Curry, Green and Thompson in a best-of-seven series.

Two of them came before they found their championship stride — the 2013 San Antonio Spurs in the West semifinals and the 2014 LA Clippers in the first round. Both caught the Warriors' burgeoning stars while young and inexperienced.

Both had a hand in teaching them valuable lessons about winning, lessons that would groom the Warriors' anchors into champions.

"As early as my second year," Thompson said when asked when he knew they would be special. "We were so young. We took on an experienced, dynastic San Antonio team in a hard-fought series. After that, I was like: 'Gosh, we're going toe-to-toe with Tim Duncan, Tony Parker and Manu Ginobili. If we build on this, we could have a great future.' For us to acquire Andre that next summer, we went through some growing pains still in 2014, but I could feel it. We were just in our early 20s."

The third loss came to the 2016 Cleveland Cavaliers in the finals, and that required Curry being limited by a sprained knee, Green getting suspended for a pivotal Game 5, injuries to key role players Iguodala and Andrew Bogut — and, of course, masterful performances by LeBron, Kyrie and Cavs coach Tyronn Lue.

None of this is a slight to the Warriors' playoff opponents. The 2019 Toronto Raptors were rightful champions, as injuries are part of surviving the postseason gauntlet. But it does provide perspective on just how special this Warriors core has been, and still is. Whenever they do lose a playoff series, it is looking less like an indictment on them and more a boon to the legacy of whoever beat them. If the Celtics or Heat knock off the Warriors in the 2022 NBA Finals, they'd join an exclusive group.

But before looking ahead to potentially their fourth championship, Curry, Green and Thompson should rightfully be celebrated. They're in their 30s now, with the scars and gray hairs to prove it. They have a new cast around them. Yet they made the finals again. After kicking the tires on a few stars, before ultimately stocking up on youth and veteran journeymen, the Warriors leaned in on their three stalwarts. They banked on them still being formidable while bringing along unproven role players. They didn't sign a big man, didn't pick up a veteran on the buyout market. The whole time, this season was riding on their big three still being top-shelf. They were.

This time, they did it against a league they created. Curry, Green and Thompson changed the NBA. Teams followed their blueprint to dominance —

the 3-point shooting, the switching defense, the agile-power forwards as centers, the long-armed athletic wings. Few teams embodied the NBA the Warriors created as much as Dallas. The Mavericks play with five shooters, have no true center and are led by an incredible point guard who can shoot.

Even in the East, Golden State's imprint is present. So if the Warriors win a title, they will have changed the league and then conquered the league they inspired.

"I think they're a really unique trio just in terms of how they complement one another in every way," Kerr said. "They're such different players. Draymond is kind of our point forward. He's the best defender in the league. He's our emotional leader. Steph and Klay already established themselves as this amazing shooting backcourt. But they needed each other from the beginning. Klay (handled) some of the tougher defensive assignments to allow Steph to be able to focus more on the offensive end. Then the three of them together, the way they move the ball, they pass and cut. It's beautiful to watch."

During the offseason of 2021, all three of the Warriors' core recruited Iguodala to return to the Bay Area. They wanted their "super vet," as Green calls him. They told him they needed him to get back to the mountaintop. Curry promised endless rounds of golf.

It was Iguodala who first saw the potential in them. Before even the Warriors did. He faced them in that 2013 series against Denver and learned live what was so special about them. He orchestrated his way to the Warriors, and his arrival elevated their games.

In many ways, Iguodala was the beta for what this trio could be.

He was the first player to show talent could fit with them. He was an All-Star who came to the Warriors before any of the three were. Green was still a reserve, and Thompson was just stepping into his role as the Robin to Curry's Batman, a role David Lee previously held until he got injured in their first postseason. It was their joy that lured Iguodala. How they simultaneously shined and sacrificed. How they were hoopers at their core

and preoccupied with winning. How they always had space at the table for anyone looking to feast with them.

Iguodala was the spark that led to Shaun Livingston and Leandro Barbosa. And eventually Kevin Durant, Zaza Pachulia and David West. And now the renovation of Andrew Wiggins and Otto Porter Jr.

"I think the ability to set the table for pretty much anybody that comes in," Curry said, "be a part of the fold, find their way, elevate their game, take that next step wherever they are in their career — I think we pride ourselves on that more than what we do individually. Because you got a lot of examples of guys that have been elsewhere and come here and found success. To be able to do it on the biggest of stages, that's not easy to do. ... We found a way to create the culture that it starts with us, but everybody else gets to eat, too. I guess that's the fun part."

In Chase Center on a Thursday night, the fun was beginning.

It was Green hoisting the Oscar Robertson Trophy for the Western Conference champions while his teammates converged on him to get a hand on the hardware.

It was Green hoisting Curry when the point guard was given the Magic Johnson Award as Western Conference finals MVP.

It was Thompson, being hoisted as the hero of the night. Beneath roars from the crowd dipped in yellow, the color of happiness, Thompson got emotional trying to explain his joy. If anyone can speak to the doubt about his ability to get back here, it's him. If anyone can appreciate the significance of them making it this far, it's him. On this night, Thompson, whose absence was responsible for the Warriors' postseason hiatus, exemplified the excellence of this Warriors trio. A rendering of their greatness. An illustration of their tenacity. A portrait of their capacity.

If you take a step back and view them from a wider perspective, you'll see the masterpiece Iguodala sees. Appreciation will follow. ▬

This book is available in quantity at special discounts for your group or organization.
For further information, contact:

Triumph Books LLC
814 North Franklin Street
Chicago, Illinois 60610
Phone: (312) 337-0747
www.triumphbooks.com

Printed in U.S.A.
ISBN: 978-1-63727-238-1

The Athletic

Paul Fichtenbaum, Chief Content Officer
Dan Kaufman, Editorial Director
Chris Sprow, Editorial Director
Evan Parker, SVP/GM Content Operations
Sergio Gonzalez, Senior Managing Editor - NBA
Tyler Batiste, Managing Editor - NBA
Zachary Pierce, National Managing Editor
Jenny Dial Creech, Deputy Managing Editor - NBA
Sunaya Sapurji, Senior Editor - NBA
Joan Niesen, Staff Editor - NBA
Oscar Murillo, VP Design
Wes McCabe, Design Director
Kenny Dorset, Social Engagement
Trevor Gibbons, Partnerships Director
Jenna Winchell, Marketing Director
Casey Malone, Associate CRM Director
Amanda Ephrom, Brand Strategist
Tyler Sutton, Marketing Manager
Ankur Chawla, Business Development
Brooks Varni, Editorial Operations
Rosalie Pisano, Partnerships Manager
Martin Oppegaard, Programming Manager
Christy Aumer, Marketing Operations

Featured writers from The Athletic
Sam Amick, Rustin Dodd, Jayson Jenks, Tim Kawakami, Anthony Slater, Marcus Thompson II, Joe Vardon

Special thanks to the entire The Athletic NBA Staff

Content packaged by Mojo Media, Inc.
Joe Funk: Editor
Jason Hinman: Creative Director

Unless otherwise noted, all interior photos by AP Images